.

Straight Talk from the Heartland

An Entrepreneur's Memoir

Other books by John Torinus Jr:

The Company That Solved Health Care (2010)

The Grassroots Revolution in Health Care (2013)

Straight Talk from the Heartland

An Entrepreneur's Memoir

John Torinus Jr.

Henschel HAUS
www.henschelHAUSbooks.com
Milwaukee, Wisconsin

Photos courtesy of the author.

Published by
HenschelHAUS Publishing, Inc.
Milwaukee, Wisconsin
www.henschelHAUSbooks.com

ISBN (paperback): 978159598–791-4
ISBN (hardcover): 978159598–872-0
E-ISBN: 978159598-794-5
LCCN: 2020946606

Printed in the United States of America

"To those who are given much, much is expected."
— Maya Angelou

"Contribute as much as you can to the end,
until there is no more to give."
— John Torinus Jr.

Table of Contents

To entrepreneurs
— for-profit and non-profit —
who make the world better,
smarter, and more prosperous.

GRANDPA AND DAD
JOURNALISTS BEFORE ME

"V.I." Victor Minahan left his law practice in 1914 to start and buy newspapers in Green Bay and Appleton, Wisconsin. They were a major success. My step-grandfather wrote daily editorials until he died in 1954. He was the publisher of both the *Green Bay Press Gazette* and the *Appleton Post Crescent.*

My dad, John Torinus, known as "Tor," went to work for the *Green Bay Press-Gazette* right out of Dartmouth College, where he ran the student newspaper. He returned to the newsroom as an editor after serving in World War II, ending as a lieutenant colonel. He wrote columns and editorials for five decades and was also general manager. He wrote a seminal history of the Green Bay Packers: *The Packer Legend: An Inside Look.*

CHAPTER 1

Everyone Has a Story — Here's Mine
ONE FOOT IN THE GAME, ONE ON SIDELINES

Journalists, like me, my father and grandfather before me and two brothers, soon learn that everybody has a story. I have always been fascinated with other people's stories. I read obits. Countless times have I wished my forebears had recorded their stories so I could connect with them and our family's journey. It is in that spirit that I write my part of that tale. This memoir is an imperfect lens on my journey and the times I lived in.

After 50-plus years as a reporter, editorial writer, columnist, book writer, speaker and blogger, I won't pass on this opportunity to voice an occasional opinion. I guesstimate that I wrote about 4,000 editorials or columns, mostly columns, in a half-century of journalism. I'd like to think they had some impact at the time, realizing fully that real advances are brought about by doers, not observers. I like to think a journalist's perishable writings blend into an important dialog for the making of a better community and state. I played the role of a thought gatherer and analyst on the local level and later on at higher levels on some issues. The bedrock for a healthy community, state, or country is good information and healthy dialog, usually offered through newspapers.

When I left my last gig as a full-time journalist and business editor of *The Milwaukee Sentinel* in 1987, one of my fellow editors at the paper was asked by a reporter if I would have made a good editor for the newspaper. My colleague and competitor for the top job said, "Torinus is more of a player than an observer." He was right. I was never completely at home on the sidelines. Imprinted indelibly by my grandfather and father, I had always aspired to be a publisher of a newspaper, a position that can combine writing with leadership. I came close in West Bend, Wisconsin, where I was general manager and editor. But I was a hired hand, not the publisher or owner. I don't have many regrets about missing out on the life my father and grandfather lived, even though I thought it was my calling. Some things are not meant to be. You adapt.

My childhood neighbor and life-long friend, Johnny Brogan, a boisterous Irish-American politician who lived his life in the New Deal long after the New Deal had passed, kept me grounded. Over a bourbon or two or three, he observed, "Writing editorials is like peeing in your blue serge suit: You feel warm all over, and no one notices." Thanks, Johnny.

The other bromide about editorial writers says, "They are the guys who come down from the hills after the battle is over and shoot the wounded."

In response to such reverence, I took two tacks:

- My brother Tom and I jettisoned the time-honored anonymous editorials in our newspapers and replaced them with personal columns. We shed the safety of the wizard behind the editorial curtain. Our photos headed our opinion pieces. We were transparent and accountable. The personal touch worked as it had for many years for "Tor," our father, who had a large following. (Dad's first Sunday column when he took over as editor of the *Appleton Post-Crescent* was the defense of straight martinis versus martinis on the rocks, which he called "martini punch.") He did 50 years as a journalist and columnist. By the end so did I, with a few breaks in between.

1. Everyone Has a Story — Here's Mine

- After 20 years in newsrooms, I chose to live a more engaged life, as opposed to that of an objective journalist. News people do their work from the outside looking in. They observe, probe, sometimes analyze, and record. They are seldom insiders. Having run businesses, served in the military, worked in politics, dug sewers, lectured at university, led non-profit organizations and served on dozens of boards, I had the distinct advantage of being an insider. Most journalists are rookies when it comes to real world experience. Scar tissue gave me a leg up on my fellow pundits. An engaged life does create conflicts and biases, but at least you know something whereof you speak. It is true that you can't write about some things when you are on the inside looking out. There are confidences, conflicts of interest and proprieties. On balance, though, save me from an antiseptic life without conflicts. Being insulated from real action is the Achilles heel of journalists and intellectuals.

My bent for starting businesses and non-profit organizations got its beginnings as an "intrapreneur" for Wisconsin newspapers. The first was a piggyback daily for the Neenah-Menasha market, then an new daily built off an old weekly paper in West Bend, and finally, a string of 13 weeklies in the Milwaukee suburbs. The first two succeeded; the weekly competitors to *The Milwaukee Journal* and *Sentinel* failed. I learned a lot about the joys and agonies of starting an enterprise, and I repeated the experience many times.

A life of action led to a differentiating dimension in my writings. News people are experts at illuminating problems and issues in society. Academics are too, but they were never trained to be problem solvers. My training in management was always about problem solving. *Ergo*, in each column that dealt with an issue, I always tried to include a solution, a path forward. That put a positive touch on each column.

Straight Talk From the Heartland

When I hit my 70s, I kept writing weekly columns and blogs. My friends would ask why. I would joke that I was like a bubble machine, that I didn't know how to turn it off or that it was like flatulence in old age — it just came out. The real answer, of course, was that my writing defined me and gave me a channel for contributing.

Ideas, at least good ideas, have consequences. If you can sell them to a large enough group of Americans, they create movement toward positive changes in a world with unending challenges.

I learned with age the virtue of patience. It would often take a decade for a better concept to take root and be adopted. I was always sadly aware that the mountains of copy I ginned out over 50 years could be quickly lost in the wash of history but could have a cumulative impact. I like to think that each of us who cares is a sliver of light in a galaxy of good acts and intentions. George H. W. Bush, my favorite president, used the metaphor: "A thousand points of light" to describe a healthy country.

Brothers Tom and Mark decided to start a group of local papers in Michigan's Upper Peninsula, a nice place but not much of a market. They won walls full of journalism awards and plaques. And had a fine time with five publications before selling out. Along the way, they gave a dozen brilliant young journalists their start.

1. Everyone Has a Story — Here's Mine

The best part of life as a community journalist is that you are fully engaged. Like a country doctor, a small-town editor has intimate relationships with the people in the community. You publish birth announcements, high school sports exploits, wedding notices, the doings of the school board and city council, and the obituaries. You are connected.

My columns ran for a span of five decades in the *Appleton Post-Crescent*, the *West Bend News*, suburban papers, and the *Milwaukee Journal Sentinel*. Because of an even-handed approach to the news and the issues, I got lots of feedback and dialog, which at times served to advance or support key initiatives. Most of the feedback was positive, mainly I think because my journalism was grounded and had an element of validity. Thanks to the ubiquitous Internet, later in life I could run those ideas out on my website, *Straight Talk from the Heartland*, the title also of this memoir.

When daily newspapers took a disastrous dive in the 1990s, never to return as a dominating force, the events that had taken me out of the newsroom proved, in the end, fortuitous. My career turned out better than life as a publisher in a declining industry. I had become a rare bird: part news commentator for Wisconsin publications, part businessman, and part public policy player.

Another family shot, before Mark, the last to arrive, when Mom was 39.
From L to R: Tom, Nancy, John, Laurel, and Chuck Torinus (May 1956).

Dad was always a Pied Piper for kid adventures. A rowboat was a perfect vehicle for one.

CHAPTER 2

Sweet Times:
Growing Up in the 1940s and 1950s
PINK SHIRTS, BLUE SUEDE SHOES

O n a sunny Wisconsin summer day in 1945, my dad, Lt. Col. John B. Torinus, 82nd Airborne Division, U.S. Army, stopped abruptly while walking to Royal Cleaners in De Pere, Wisconsin to pick up pressed and starched uniforms, like the one he was wearing. He had just returned from WWII in Europe. He had my small hand in his left hand. I was eight. He snapped to a salute with his right hand as the bells started ringing from the steeples of St. Mary's and St. Francis Catholic churches in our hometown. They were tolling to celebrate the victory over Japan — VJ Day, August 14, 1945. He held the salute for what seemed like several minutes until the bells went silent.

I was proud of my dad. I realized only later that President Truman's decision to drop the bombs on Hiroshima and Nagasaki to bring the war to an end had spared Dad from re-deployment to the Asian Theater. He was on furlough after returning from the bloody European Theater, where he had served on the staff of Gen. Matthew Ridgeway. He had orders for the Far Eastern Theater.

Like most veterans who saw too much of the gruesome realities of war, he never talked much about his service. I did eke out later that his Bronze Star was awarded for dynamiting a blocked intersection in a small town in France in the summer of

7

1945 so the rapidly advancing U.S. Army could continue its race to remaining bridges over the Rhine River.

American life had been consumed by the war effort, so it was natural that the boys in our neighborhood constantly played war games in the nearby fields and woods. We also played cowboys and Indians, a vestige of the 1800s, but still Hollywood fare. Because Dad was a lieutenant colonel (when he was only 32), my brother Tom, a year younger, and I vied for officer roles in our pretend units. Bob Newell, a neighbor, usually ended up on top rank through force of personality. Tom and I got comfortable with the idea of leadership. It was ingrained.

Louise — Mom — was a leader, too, heading the Green Bay Service League and Red Cross Bloodmobile drives. She had her hands full, and then some, with a family of six kids. It was a Catholic family before the days of the pill. My parents relied on what Catholics were told to follow, the "rhythm method," an abstinence schedule. It never worked very well. Mark, a prime example, the last of four boys and two girls, was born in 1953 when Mom was 39. In between were Chuck, born at Fort Benning, GA in 1943, Laurie and Nancy in Green Bay in 1947 and 1949. I, the oldest, and brother Tom were pre-war babies, born 15 months apart in Green Bay in 1937 and 1938.

The wives of WWII servicemen have been under-appreciated by history. When Dad was assigned to Fort Benning, where the airborne forces trained, Mom packed up Tom and me and followed him from Green Bay. Our small brick bungalow on the base got a little crowded when Chuck was born. We had an African-American nanny and maid who lived with us. She was a lovely person as I recall, whose name, I am embarrassed to say, I can't remember.

Louise again packed up the three kids and followed her husband to a Rhode Island Army assignment. She did it again

2. Sweet Times: Growing Up in the 1940s and 1950s

Family of Louise and John Torinus (1961). Standing (from L): Tom, Louise, John Jr., Chuck. Seated (from L): Laurel, Mark, Nancy, John Sr.

Mom added tall white columns to our simple "salt box" home at 916 Lawton Place in East DePere, Wisconsin. The three oldest boys shared one bedroom.

Louise's 80th birthday in Bermuda (1994).From L: Kine and John, Tom, Laurel Torinus Culp, Maryclaire Torinus, Nancy, Mark, Mary, Peter Culp, Louise, and Chuck.

when he left there for the invasion of Europe. She back-tracked to De Pere, near Green Bay, to live with Grandma Bertha Minahan and V.I. (Victor Ivan), Dad's stepfather. I never heard her complain about any of it.

Louise was strong and independent, so she soon arranged to move to a new house in a nearby subdivision called Urbandale. When the men in the neighborhood came home from fighting, it became known as "Bourbandale" for good reason.

These men had seen it all: death and cruelty in overdose. They had learned to squeeze in good times whenever they could. They had survived the trauma of war, and they meant to live the rest of their lives to the fullest. They worked hard to build careers, businesses and families. Booze, mainly bourbon, and partying were a big part of their go-for-the-gusto, live-today-for-tomorrow-you-may-die culture. It was a close-knit, kid-friendly neighborhood.

Bud Newell built a backyard hockey rink for the neighborhood kids every winter. Wes "Bunny" Garner created weekly stories of long sagas about an assortment of cowboy characters for audiences of rapt children. The men built camouflaged duck hunting barges, used as mobile blinds on the west shore of Green Bay. Grace Branson taught us French.

Our fathers and mothers created "Moon Valley Ski Club" on a modest hill along Baird's Creek on the outskirts of Green Bay. It was a friendly jab at posh Sun Valley, Idaho, where only the well-off Kress family could afford to go. Our club was more fun in many ways. The fathers hauled in an old railroad depot as the warming chalet. It was heated by a cast iron potbelly stove, just right for roasting hot dogs and marshmallows after skiing. I remember Mom hovering to keep the dueling wiener and marshmallow sticks from crossing in the stove's opening. The privy was a two-hole outhouse. Our rope tows were powered by gasoline engines mounted on toboggans. A stationary electric motor came later.

Every fall, the fathers hand-spliced ropes that were hung on a series of pulleys. The rudimentary safety device was a trip wire across the exit point at the top of the hills. It saved a kid or two from the pulleys as their baggy jackets got wrapped around the rope. The dads rigged lights, and we skied into the evenings every weekend and some weekday nights. Bud Newell's sound system carried scratchy tunes, like "Red Sails in the Sunset" that got stuck and was cranked out over and over. I will never escape that melody.

Tor was the maestro of Moon Valley. He would lead the kids into the woods on cross-country treks, breaking trail, with the old cable bindings unhinged at the heel. What more could anyone want, except a few more feet on top of its 200 vertical feet?

It was skiing there weekends and nights that I fell in boyish love with Caroline "Kine" Icks, who was to become my second wife in later years. She was 10, pretty as a spring day and full of life. Her mom Margaret and my mother Louise knitted the "fast caps" that all the kids wore. Each unique cap featured a puffball attached to a six-inch braided string. We thought they made us look like hot skiers when the ball flew behind as we zipped down our runs.

We went up and down the little hill until our hands could no longer grip the rope. We had leather mitts called "choppers" that often wore out before season's end. The skiers packed the loose snow by side-stepping up hill in tandem. The ultimate challenge was the un-groomed "north slope." It was steep and hard to handle on the stiff and long wooden skis of the day. Our ski coach Ed Branson missed a gate and straddled a tree, one ski on each side. I had to cut him out of his long leather thong bindings (no safety, quick release bindings back then). He sat on an inner tube for a couple of months.

Ed and Dad taught us to race and drove our team in the Central U.S. Ski Association circuit to bigger, scary hills in the Upper Peninsula of Michigan: Iron Mountain, Rib Mountain, Houghton and Marquette. They were hardly mountains, but produced a lot of world-class skiers. My brothers Tom and Chuck went on to become college racers at Dartmouth and Regis. Kine and her sister Abett (Elizabeth) went on to become national champions in age-class cross-country skiing. Abett medaled in world competition and Kine came close.

Skiing and northern life have always been a part of who we are. Even later on in life, after retirement when our friends went south for the winter, Kine and I headed north. I skied the

2. Sweet Times: Growing Up in the 1940s and 1950s

American Birkebeiner, a 32-mile hilly marathon, or its half-marathon companion race, 30 times, 15 each. It was an annual ritual and challenge. You had to be in some semblance of shape to take on its 39 climbs. At the end of my Birkie days, the number of racers had grown to more than 12,000 — the Boston Marathon of skiing.

There was no television until we were teens, no electronic diversions, no fast food. We read lots of books, like "The Hardy Boys" series about kid detectives. We played pick-up sports all summer long, after school and on weekends. There was hockey on Reimer's Pond, basketball on Gnewuch's driveway, softball and football on the Stone's vacant lot. I broke an ankle when I stepped in a hole while playing no-pads tackle football on that lot.

That was my first of more than a dozen sports injuries, part of the deal for being active. I was a little beat up by my golden years, but in a lot better shape than the guys who weren't active.

My siblings and I were blessed with exceptional parents, and that made growing up a sweet time. Dinner for the eight of us was promptly at six every night. The food was what we could afford on Dad's journalist salary. (They were paid poorly back then, too.) We had budget meals: beef tongue casseroles, liver and onions, Kraft macaroni and cheese dinners (especially when Mom and Dad went out for dinner) and bologna. The kids almost never went out for dinner. There was always enough food to go around, but you had to hold your own at the dinner table.

The dinner conversation was always spirited. Lively conversation over a meal became my favorite activity throughout life.

Later, Mom became a gourmet cook, taking lessons in French cooking from Madame Kuony at the Postilion in Fond du Lac. The guests at her exquisite tables said Louise could have run a fine restaurant. Friends coveted her dinner invitations. So we

Louise and John, Mom and Dad, were strong, loving role models. We were so lucky.

suffered not at her table — unless our table manners were not up to her standards. Her instrument of discipline was a wooden spoon, often threatened, almost never used.

Life had an easy rhythm in small-town Wisconsin. We walked about a mile to and from St. Francis Catholic School, careful to never step on a crack in the sidewalks or "break your mother's back." The walk was also a time to store up benediction points for the hereafter by saying short prayers such as simply: "Jesus, Mary, Joseph," an inscrutable prayer indeed. We said them fast to pick up points. An active boy, I figured I should bank a bunch of them.

On the way to school, we sometimes stopped at Baeten's Bakery on George Street to purchase two sweet rolls — a long john and caramel roll. The nuns allowed them to be eaten in first hour at your desk, but only if you had gone to mass and had fasted to receive communion.

It was about third grade that I started having doubts about whether the flat wafer and red wine hoisted by our priest at the height of the mass really could be the body and blood of Jesus Christ. "Could there be transubstantiation?" I was skeptical then and remained so.

Despite heretical inklings, Tom and I served dutifully as altar boys. I loved the ritual of the mass, the symmetry of the hour-long pageant. We were taught rote Latin, so we could chime in with appropriate prayers and responses on cue. "*Sursum corda, habemus ad Dominem.*" We helped the priests don their ceremonial vestments in the sacristy. Father Bache, the parish priest, was a gentle man who led with kindly example. Never did my brothers or I see a sign of the tragic scandal between priests and boys that was to rock the Catholic Church to its core in later years.

My wife Kine pointed out that I was a grounded child, not the vulnerable type that a pedophile would seek out.

By my mid-20s, I was "black," meaning a non-practicing Catholic. The priest predator scandal convinced me more than ever before that the U.S. Catholic Church should secede from the Vatican. It could then welcome females to the priesthood and priests to marry. Catholics would then sign up in big numbers for that career, which has become a disappearing vocation. Nuns should also be able to marry and divorce.

In grade school, the nuns ruled.

The nuns at St. Frances Grade School were special people. They were teachers who devoted 100 percent of their lives and energies to teaching children how to be successful in academics and life. Sister Nona in first and second grades, Sister Felicitas in third and fourth, Sister Leonora in fifth and sixth was my favorite.

She was good, but severe and tough. Sister Vera, the stern principal, whom we carelessly nicknamed "Vicious Vera," for seventh and eighth. I remember them all fondly.

Sister Felicitas had a story, though the nuns' personalities and biographies were purposely hidden behind their habits and their cloistered lives of anonymous service to their God and duty. They were selfless and purposely faceless. Sad in a way. I would have loved to have known their narratives. We only knew them in the classroom.

Sister Felicitas, who was still teaching in her 70s and probably 80s (it was hard to discern age behind the habits), stressed math. We noticed but didn't mind when she wrote out problems with white chalk on the blackboard that her palsied hand put saw teeth in the numbers. Her story, we heard, was that she had been an heiress to the Hershey Chocolate fortune and had turned all her assets over to the Sisters of Notre Dame when she decided to leave privileged life for her vocation.

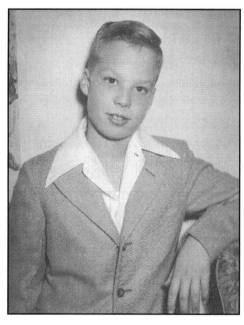

John Jr., 8th grade.

2. Sweet Times: Growing Up in the 1940s and 1950s

School agreed with me, except for what was called "deportment" on report cards. I was active and talkative. You are who you are. One year produced an "F" in that deportment category. I set a record for disciplinary "cards," which were sets of multiplication and division exercises handed out liberally for breaches of classroom etiquette and rules. My school record was 32 in one day. They were worked off in hours of detention after school.

Much of the teaching by the nuns was rote and repetitive. The nuns were good at working with active, even hyperactive, boys. We didn't use terms like "attention deficit" back then.

As I look back and compare our curriculum to that of my grandkids, it's worlds apart. There were no frills. We had almost no art, music or physical education. There were only football and basketball teams. We had the three Rs — reading, writing and arithmetic in spades.

In seventh or eighth grade, we were told that the girls in our class were going to get a half-day for sex education. Apparently, the boys didn't need it, because we didn't get the half-day off. I organized the older boys in protest. We printed signs and marched on Father Bache's rectory. (He must have chuckled, because we got our half-day off.) Even my proper Catholic mother was secretly amused and supportive. She looked sideways at home when we made the protest signs that we brandished.

It is apparent in retrospect that the church believed the principal responsibility for governing sexual activity rested with the girls. Not growing up on a farm where those things were a part of daily life, I was pretty much ignorant of the biology of reproduction. In college, I figured it out by reading Dr. Alex Comfort's *Loving Free. Peyton Place*, a hot title for all of us in the 1950s, helped. Incredibly, the guys at Yale were reading it for enlightenment in matters sexual. Hugh Hefner and *Playboy* came along a little too late for us.

My mother tried to educate us on the subject. She read a book to me on the birds and bees, but stopped short of the reproductive finale. I never made the full connection to boys and girls until much later. She did her best. (Where was Dad on that subject?)

Flashing forward, I made the determination that I would make sure that my two sons knew the score. The instruction books were better than in the 1950s, but they still showed Mom and Dad in bed under the covers. I explained the process fully to them. I wondered how my sons would manage those conversations with their children.

My finest hour in grade school involved Jerry Stadler, a tough farm kid, our eighth-grade fullback and the schoolyard bully. He intimidated everybody. When the kids played pom-pom pull-away at recess, he would stand in the middle of the blacktop playground and menace the rest of us. One day, I waited until he wasn't looking and launched a full speed tackle from his blind side. I flattened him. He got up, mad as hell, and I ran faster than I ever had before. It was a clean get-away, and Jerry was never quite as menacing again.

Aside from school, sports and family, a good part of the upbringing of the Torinus clan revolved around scouting. Uncle John Walter, a WWII Army officer veteran, was scoutmaster of Troop 6 at Grace Lutheran Church in Green Bay and he recruited me, Tom and Chuck. Mom was den mother of Pack 6 when we were Cub Scouts. Later, we would hitchhike the five miles to Green Bay from De Pere for weekly Boy Scout meetings. Safety was never a major issue in the 1940s and 1950s. After the meetings, we stopped at Dehn's Ice Cream on Mason Street before catching a ride home.

We got our early lessons in values and leadership in those scouting years, moving from den and patrol leader to troop leader.

2. Sweet Times: Growing Up in the 1940s and 1950s

Tom, Mark and I became Eagle Scouts and Chuck made Life Scout. We made Order of the Arrow, a camper award that involved an intimidating Native American induction ceremony and a night in the woods on your own.

Our summer camp, Bear Paw near Mountain, Wisconsin, was a beautiful place on a northern lake, one of 15,000 left by the glacier in the state. The camp is a simple place with tents and cots on wooden platforms as sleeping quarters and a common mess hall. (Dad later led a capital campaign, with my help in southern Wisconsin, to refurbish the aging structures. A building is named after him.) We learned canoeing, lifesaving, bird watching, botany, camaraderie and a lasting appreciation for the outdoors and the natural world.

A woman friend told me that when she considered marriage for the second time, she was going to find a former Eagle Scout. Her second husband asked her if she would settle for 4-H. She knew about the values instilled in those youth organizations. The Torinus boys and sister Laurie all turned out to be community leaders, and scouting surely had something to do with that outcome.

It still surprises me that my parents let me make the pivotal decision, at 14, on whether to go to a public or private high school. The local Catholic high school was male only, partly because it served as a pre-seminary for boys interested in the priesthood. I opted initially for East De Pere High School and co-education.

The freshman year at the public school offered general math and shop, and somehow I knew I needed more than that. (Besides, hands-on work was never an interest.) So, I quickly transferred to all male St. Norbert High School, where most of the classes were taught by "frats." They were fraters (Latin for brothers) who were earning PhDs, so they could teach in the Norbertine colleges, including St. Norbert's on the same campus in De Pere.

I paid the price for the academic rigor of St. Norbert's High School and no girls. For a long, long time, I was extremely shy around girls, socially awkward, maybe because I liked them so much.

I just couldn't bring myself to ask a girl for a date, or even a dance at the Catholic Youth Organization dances in Green Bay at the Catholic Women's Club. I'd go, but by the time I'd get the nerve to ask a girl to dance, the music had stopped — even with Kine, my Moon Valley ski buddy. There she was, in a pink cashmere sweater and a string of pearls, my dream girl. And I couldn't ask. I just stood there and pined. I was a total 1950s "dork," an appropriate label of the times.

Teens conformed back then like they always do and I had the right look: a flat-top crew cut, charcoal pants, pink shirt, and even blue suede shoes. Some guys at "Nubbie's" sported DAs (duck's ass haircuts), with a flat top and long, slicked hair on the sides, swept back to a curly tail in the back, like the feathers of a drake mallard. Actor James Dean was the epitome of cool, with a DA and a pack of cigarettes rolled up in the short sleeve of a white T-shirt.

Mint-green shirts replaced pink a few years later and I had one of those, too. But, the right clothes didn't make me a suave young man.

Those were the years with easy summers depicted in the movie *Picnic* with Kim Novak and James Dean. We went to dances at Bay Beach Park at the mouth of the Fox River where it empties into Green Bay. The nights were balmy and romantic, like in *Picnic*, but not for me. They were torture, fumbling around on the sidelines, too shy to participate.

2. Sweet Times: Growing Up in the 1940s and 1950s

There were a few male rumbles back then, especially at the beer bars, where 18-year-olds could drink legally, and even younger teens would use fake IDs. A lot of my friends sneaked into Mercer's, a beer bar in Green Bay. I missed that scene, because I never drank in high school. Just wasn't interested.

It was the age of hot rods, when teenage boys fixed their own cars and "souped" them up. More of a dreamer, I didn't get around to getting my license until a year after the legal driving age of 16.

I did trigger one rumble in my senior year. Somehow, I stumbled into a date with Katie Burr, a lovely red-headed sophomore cheerleader for Green Bay East High. It was their homecoming and I got the bright idea to wear my letter sweater showing a big green "N" front and center. Three football players wearing red East letter sweaters, including Lloyd Basten and Ozzie Piaskowski, both all-state backs, jumped me on the way out of the dance. We scuffled to the ground, I had Ozzie in a headlock and then somehow it was over, no harm done. I can't remember if Katie was impressed.

Flash forward 51 years to Kine's 50th East High class reunion. In the days before, I told Kine I was going to settle the score with Ozzie, whom Kine had dated in high school. Heh, heh.

Arriving at the reunion in Green Bay, where I knew only a few people, I braced myself with a whiskey Manhattan. While the bartender mixed, I noticed this guy with no neck and a flat top giving me a hard look from 30 feet away. I manned up, took a stiff swig and walked over.

Said I: "Do you know who I am?"

Said he: "I know who you are."

We stiffly shake hands.

Said I: "What did you end up doing, Ozzie?"

"I joined the Marine Corps, John, made a career of it."

"I was in the Marine Corps, Ozzie."

"No shit!!"

Man-hugs.

We talked all night.

The fraters were great teachers and my entire class had only 44 students, so the classes were personal and effective. My senior physics class had three students.

Algebra and the obligatory Latin were offered freshman year, followed by advanced algebra, geometry and trigonometry. Back then, calculus wasn't taught in high school. I opted out of fourth year Latin, to the dismay of the Norbertines.

Discipline was high, and I often had to spend Sunday afternoons in "study hall" detention to work off demerits for hijinks. For some strange reason, the priests in charge made you just sit there; study was not allowed. I guess the punishment was utter boredom.

I'm still embarrassed by some of my disrespectful pranks. I set the desk of Frat Jacobs on the very edge of the elevated platform in the front of the classroom, taking advantage of his habit of hopping up there at the beginning of class. He flew into the second row. Why would I think that was funny? Jacobs flailed at my fellow prankster, Tommy Johnson, and the good frater's watch flew in parts across the room. Demerits followed.

Mostly, it was a serious place and I thrived there, editing the yearbook, serving as class officer most years, graduating at the top of the small class.

The Torinus men seem to mature later than most physically, so I was undistinguished in football as a guard and center linebacker. Our team won several state championships, including my senior year. Johnson, our little halfback, who went on to be a blackjack dealer in Las Vegas, was all-state. All the seniors were first or second team all-league, except me at honorable mention.

2. Sweet Times: Growing Up in the 1940s and 1950s

But I was team captain, not afraid to be vocal when necessary and liking leadership. "Get your butt in there, Tomasini," was my repeated challenge for our 225-pound imported tackle from Milwaukee.

The challenge for me at pulling guard in front of Johnson from our head coach, Fred Dillon, was, "Torinus, get the piano off your back." Speed was not my long suit.

Dillon was a gruff but funny bachelor with a prodigious nose, who lived upstairs at the Union Hotel in downtown De Pere. He gave other players swift boots in the rear.

Other teachers were not shy about corporal punishment either. As evidence, there is still a floating bone chip in my right shin from a swift kick delivered by our physics teacher, Frater Conway. He didn't appreciate my humor.

Because there were fewer resources and not so many options for people after the war, times were simpler. Dad often hitchhiked five miles to work from De Pere to the *Green Bay Press-Gazette* so Mom could use the family car. The Torinus boys walked or biked a mile-and-a-half to St. Norbert's High School in West De Pere across the Fox River. We, too, sometimes hitched rides.

There was a Torinus boy at St. Norbert's for 22 years. The education there got three of us into Ivy League colleges and one into UW–Madison.

We were well enough off, so we didn't have to have jobs during the school year, but we worked in the summers. I peddled my one-speed bike to my farm job about three miles up Scray's Hill on the ledge, a prehistoric limestone sedimentary escarpment that forms Door County and continues east to become Niagara Falls. I made 50 cents an hour working for George Baker, a close family friend who ran a turkey farm for a few years. (I climbed that escarpment many times in later years on multispeed bicycles.)

A turkey gains one-quarter of a pound for every pound of consumed food. My job was to feed the birds and shovel the other three-quarters of each pound. I bulked up some for football by lifting bales of hay.

Another next-door neighbor, Bob Chapel, hired me as a laborer at his underground sewer and water construction company. I worked alongside his regular guys and sometimes next to my best friend, his son Caleb. The pay was great at $2 an hour.

Caleb and I got into scuba diving in old water-filled quarries around Green Bay and that skill set allowed us to do some underwater construction work on water intake pipes. The Chapels hired me whenever I was back home, even after my graduate degree. The work kept me in cash. After college, Bob Chapel asked me to join the firm, but it was Caleb's deal, not mine.

I learned a lot working in construction, like how to become invisible when the union organizers came around to gain a membership and collect union dues. I hid inside the big pipes.

I spoke some Swedish after my two-year graduate stint at the University of Stockholm. The local guys on a crew in Escanaba in the Upper Peninsula of Michigan didn't know that, and I let them go on making smart remarks in Swedish about those two college guys in the trench. Then I started a conversation in their language. That was a major league "gotcha," but the only time I ever put that language to work after Sweden.

The work was hard, but I liked physical labor. For each exertion, there is a visible accomplishment, unlike more abstract lines of work. Maybe that's one reason I took to newspapering. There is a tangible product at the end of each workday — less enduring, though, than a sewer line.

One other lesson: avoid busting into old sewer pipes, which happened too often. No explanation necessary.

2. Sweet Times: Growing Up in the 1940s and 1950s

"RICH AND PRIVILEGED" HALF TRUE

When I left the *Milwaukee Sentinel*, I smarted at a *Milwaukee Magazine* profile in 1987 that portrayed me as having come from a "rich and privileged" background. Monetarily, it was simply wrong, though educationally, socially, and emotionally, it was true. I called the reporter, a friend, and reminded him that my dad was a journalist, so we were far from rich. We were solidly middle class.

But, on reflection, I had to concede that my three brothers and two sisters and I were, indeed, privileged. There is no greater privilege than to be blessed with stable, loving parents.

Louise Bambenek Torinus, our mother, was a class act all her long life. And John Bush Torinus, our father, was a robust, dynamic and attentive dad. Dad lost his bearings to alcohol, dishevelment, and trysts in his last decade, but he was full of life and positive leadership for most of his days. He pulled us into his fun-loving and creative orbit. His energy and high spirit were our sun. I choose to remember his many good years. Louise was our bedrock and best role model.

EDITORIAL POSTSCRIPT

The greatest gift that can be bestowed on a life is having two stable, loving parents. The parents don't have to be perfect; they just need to be there in a loving, responsible way. They need to be reliable, one of my favorite adjectives about people I love and like. Having one unreliable parent can be overcome. Minus two means a rough road ahead. My siblings and I were privileged and blessed with two exceptional, reliable parents. That's privilege.

Mom and Dad added a family room with a long, built-in couch to accommodate their six kids. It was the center of many family activities. From L to R: Mom, Mark, John, Laurie, Chuck, Tom, Dad, and Nancy. Mostly we stayed close throughout our lives.

CHAPTER 3

"Bull Dog, Bull Dog,
Bow Wow Wow,
Eli Yale!"
PAINTING THE PRINCETON CANNON BLUE

There was no guidance counselor at St. Norbert's High School, so I remember talking to "Choo-Choo" about college. Father Clabots, our principal, loved trains and traveled the hallways chewing on an unlit cigar and making train noises. He had worked on the rails in his earlier years. Hence his nickname.

He shoved a brochure across his cluttered desk that explained a scholarship through the Naval Reserve Officer Training Corps (NROTC). With a grandfather, father and two uncles as veteran officers, I liked the idea of the military. It was a full scholarship, including books, tuition, room and board with $50 per month in expenses.

My dad, a Dartmouth grad, must have subtly planted the Ivy League seed. He never pushed it. College planning was no big deal back then and we didn't even address it until early in my senior year. Foolishly, in retrospect, I applied to only two colleges and luckily got accepted at Yale and Dartmouth. I picked Yale, never having been there, because I landed the NROTC scholarship there and Dartmouth didn't have NROTC. The full ride scholarship required three years of service after graduation.

Straight Talk From the Heartland

In addition, my paternal grandparents, V.I. and Bertha Bush Torinus Minahan, had set up an educational trust to pay for unlimited college education for their grandchildren. So I didn't really need the scholarship. (I used the trust later for grad school.) The NROTC scholarship was worth about $10,000 per year, a lot of money back then, so it lightened the load on the trust, which paid for the education of 16 grandchildren. Eventually, there were a bunch of master's degrees and one doctorate. My parents created a similar fund, education being the best of all gifts for their children and grandchildren. My two sons and 13 cousins got the gift of free education. Together, they earned 11 master's degrees. Following that tradition, I have provided funds in other forms for the educations of my four grandchildren.

Anything "free" draws over-use, so my siblings and I had to learn how to govern the trust. The education had to be degree-oriented. Photography classes in Paris are nice, but not on the trust. After a number of dropouts, we learned to pay at the completion of a semester. Otherwise, we were quite liberal in the choice of schools, majors, switches in majors, grades and time-lines. The concept that the best inheritance is a quality education has proved out in our family. No one debates that a highly educated person has a huge leg up on life.

Yale was an imposing place for a naïve lad from a small town in Wisconsin. One of the enduring strengths of Yale has been that it admitted boys, and later girls, from towns across the nation, many with scholarships, who made up 40 percent of the student body when I was there. It took us a while to catch up with the prep school grads, who had been taught in college-like programs, but we did.

I got off the plane in New Haven, Connecticut in a powder blue suit (not Yale Blue) with wide lapels. Mother had helped me pick it out at Stiefel's Men's Shop in downtown Green Bay. It

3. Bull Dog, Bull Dog, Bow, Wow, Wow, Eli Yale!

was a significant expense for the family. Off the plane and on campus, I took one look at the uniform of the day at Yale, khaki pants and tweed jackets, and called Mom in a minor panic. She authorized a replacement, a J. Press Harris tweed, grey and black. It was my only jacket; I wore it all four years.

I love that story because Mom was a very sophisticated woman. She had exquisite taste. We laughed together about that powder blue choice many times over the years.

There was something for everyone at Yale. It offered a banquet of academics and extracurriculars. Though undistinguished at football in high school, and most other sports, I loved mixing it up. I was hardly an imposing lineman at 200 pounds and just under six feet, but I decided to walk on for freshman football. Big mistake. It went OK for about four weeks until I ran into Alex Kroll at linebacker. He stopped my blocks with his hands, my feet spinning in the turf. So, after a month of drubbings, I made the wise decision to walk off, partly because of the demands of my engineering and business curriculum. I decided to be a student first and athlete at the intramural level second. The coaches didn't try to change my decision.

Kroll went on to punch out a math professor, bust his jaw in three places and get kicked out of Yale. He transferred to Rutgers, where he starred, made All-American and then played a couple of years in the NFL for the New York Giants. "A real Neanderthal," I thought at the time. Kroll went on to head one of the major ad agencies in New York.

Yale was tough. My freshman roommate who was said to have an IQ of 160, flunked out at semester. At the quarter, I got a 65 in Psychology 1 and it shocked the hell out of me. I did a paper that posited that physical appearances, such as height and looks, figured into a person's success in life and leadership. The professor ridiculed the concept and gave me the low grade. Of course, later psychological studies proved my unproved hunch to be right on. I never said it was the only dimension that counted. The grade was an alarm bell, and I worked harder. That usually works and it did in my case.

Yale was a grind, but I didn't mind. After morning and early afternoon classes, many of us studied late into the night. We hit the books many hours on weekends.

I took to courses in science, math, accounting and economics. There was nothing to suggest that journalism was to be one of my callings. I surprised myself by graduating *magna cum laude* and made Tau Beta Pi, the science and engineering equivalent of Phi Beta Kappa. I had grown to love learning and the rigor of critical thinking.

A lesser accomplishment was my quintessential sophomore prank that landed me in jail for a night in Princeton, New Jersey. Three of us decided to paint the Princeton cannon Yale Blue the night before our big football game. We were caught blue-handed, literally, on our way out of town. My dad thought it was funny when the judge assigned us a 10,000-word essay on the rights of public property. He ran the story on the front page of the *Green Bay Press-Gazette*. Mother was mortified. I carried a misdemeanor on my resume for years.

The sad part of my Yale years was that I left that fine school in a relatively uneducated state. NROTC courses, including one great course on the history of war, filled my electives, so I was long on business and engineering skills, short on all the rest, the liberal arts. That was a hole that had to be filled later in life. In retrospect, I wish I had been in a five-year program.

Yale promoted academics more than leadership. Yet, I did confirm at Yale that my aptitude and appetite for leadership were part of my make-up. I was no super-star on campus. I was awarded two epaulet bars in the midshipman corps. Roommate and close friend Pete Ulrich was the four bar leader of the corps. I organized the intramural football team at Timothy Dwight College (TD), a residential campus of about 300 young men. (We beat our counterpart college at Harvard my senior year.) And I was voted TD student council chair. That routinely led to the Mott Wooley Cup for the outstanding TD senior.

Council chair had its benefits. One was being picked to squire TD's visiting dignitaries around the campus. The Chubb Scholar in my senior year was Harry Truman and the former president was a delight. I was too busy with the logistics to realize that I had a unique journalistic opportunity to probe into the thinking of this unique man—the president who made the call to drop atomic bombs on Hiroshima and Nagasaki in 1945, only 14 years earlier. It was that controversial decision that kept my dad from reporting to the Pacific Theater. I could have probed that decision with Truman, but was too obtuse to seek that level of engagement with a historic, yet approachable man.

We did have some fun at Yale. It wasn't in the boy-girl realm, because there were few women around. There were a few mixers, but they were awkward. Some guys found time to do the fraternity thing and visited the women's Ivy colleges. Don't know how they managed the time.

The fun was in intramural sports, great conversation at all meals and some drinking on weekends. One Friday night, we were drinking and cavorting, letting off steam and Pete Ulrich donned his fencing gear and began cutting large swatches of air in our dorm room. Inaccurately, he sliced my tall martini pitcher in half. He went on to be one of the leaders of NASA. Pete told me at our 50th reunion he didn't remember the incident. No surprise there.

Pete didn't act like it, but he was the superstar in our group. He led the midshipman corps, played bass in a jazz group and graduated magna cum laude in physics. He went on to a PhD in optical physics from MIT and spent most of his career at NASA, where he managed the Hubble Telescope program. He led the team that made the Cassini shot to the rings of Saturn. I tried several times to convince class leaders to have Pete give his insights on space exploration for our reunions' menu of lectures, to no avail. Go figure. The prep school guys mostly run class affairs. I couldn't get on the podium, either, though health care economics was often a topic and I had written two books on the subject. Pete and I lost touch during our careers, but we and our wives, Kine and Jeanne, reconnected at our 40th reunion and stayed close thereafter. After retiring from NASA, Pete turned to painting and teaching watercolors; he was also gifted at that. A modest man, his business card reads: "Peter Ulrich — Watercolorist."

After he retired, Pete let me write a column on his views on space exploration. In the aftermath of the successful Apollo 11 landing on the moon in 1969, he opposed further such expeditions by humans. Unmanned probes would be far safer and effective in his view. That strategy carried the day for 50 years.

The TD crew occasionally escaped on weekends. I was a guest of the families of my Jewish roommates: Steve Kranz of Scarsdale, New York; Larry Climo of New Haven (lots of warm embraces at both). It was also hosted by the families of Bob Burn of Montclair, New Jersey and Vic Tremblay of Concord, New Hampshire. I didn't have the discretionary dough to get home during the school year, except at Christmastime when a bunch of us Midwesterners would drive straight through for 20 hours. So the warmth from my friends' families was most welcome. Vic, an NROTC buddy, and I skied the New England mountains. We hunted grouse near Concord, New Hampshire, where his parents ran a small grocery store. We were like brothers.

3. Bull Dog, Bull Dog, Bow, Wow, Wow, Eli Yale!

I made the trek to Dartmouth several times to ski with brother Tom, who was a year behind me. Dick Egan, two years behind at Yale and from my hometown, had access to a car. Five of us piled in with skis for the Dartmouth Winter Carnival and a visit to Tom's fraternity. We passed a carload of girls headed up the freeway to the same destination and held up a note inviting them for a chat. They flirted a bit but must have had Dartmouth boys on their minds. They declined with a lipstick message on their window. How to respond? Vic Tremblay rolled down the front-seat window and mooned them at 75 miles an hour as we passed. Perfect. We slept in the car that night after consuming a case of very cheap "Bullfrog Beer." The air was unbreathable.

Vic was one of those gifted guys who drew all the high cards. He did well in biochemistry without cracking the books much. A good looking Italian American, he found the girls where there were none. There was often a tie on the door, meaning I had to find another place to rack for the night. Vic wanted to be a Navy pilot in the worst way. In our NROTC orientation flight out of Corpus Christi, Texas, when the pilots were diving and rolling to see if the midshipman in the back seat could handle the gravity changes, Vic heaved his cookies. He was out as a pilot. I held mine, but opted for the Marines instead.

Vic spent ten years on surface ships and became a banker. He was the first of our tight group of friends to pass away. I had tried to maintain his connection with our group from Timothy Dwight, but career setbacks along with health issues seemed to take the life out of Vic, and he withdrew. The rest of us worked to stay connected and remained good friends. Most made it to our 55th reunion. Our wives became friends. That has proved to be one of the best parts of Yale, those lifelong friendships. Kine and I decided that reunions were not to be missed.

The necrology of our Class of 1959, a list of our departed classmates at the 55th reunion, recorded only 200 among the departed. We were all about 76 at that reunion, about the average life span for an American male in 2014. So, by normal numbers, half of us, or 522 of a class of 1043, should have died by then. Our positive necrological outcome would suggest a connection between a good education and longevity.

As life will have it, only Bob Burn and Ken and Sally Warman from our group made the 60th reunion. Kine and I had a wonderful time interacting with the still intellectually curious classmates and their wives. The dialogue with classmates was the best part of my education at Yale.

A requirement of an NROTC scholarship is an eight-week summer training program. After my sophomore year in 1958, my assignment as a midshipman was a tour on the famous battle-ship *Iowa*. I worked on its nine 16-inch guns loading 50-pound bags of gun powder in their breeches. The explosives hurled huge projectiles up to 38 miles. The ship steamed 24 hours a day. Watches came at all hours; you learned to catch cat naps whenever you could. Three thousand men manned this marvel of engineering.

3. Bull Dog, Bull Dog, Bow, Wow, Wow, Eli Yale!

EDITORIAL POSTSCRIPT

I loved Yale and never worked harder in my life than the first three years there. But I concluded after graduation that I was an uneducated man. My course load was like a double major in engineering and business, and almost all my electives were filed with requirements for my Naval ROTC scholarship. There was one great "history of war" course that could have counted as liberal arts, but I missed the grand buffet of offerings in literature, philosophy, language and the arts that Yale offers. In retrospect, my education journey should have been five years instead of four. I had to fill in my educational gaps by reading and eventually taking a master's degree in political science and economics. The take-home: in a full life, learning never ends—nor should it. The day you stop learning is the day you start checking out of life.

 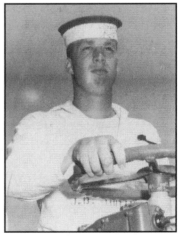

L: As a newly commissioned second lieutenant in the U.S. Marine Corps, I was still greener than grass. But I was bestowed with a ceremonial "swagger stick." I had a modicum of swagger as I posed behind a Yale fence. That might have been the last time I used it.
R: Manning a 20-millimeter gun as a midshipman on the battleship *Iowa* in 1958.

John and Tom at the Omelet.

Dad was stationed at Fort Benning, Georgia, as a training officer before being shipped out to Europe prior to the grand invasion of the continent. We lived in a small, on-base house. Brother Chuck was born at Fort Benning. Mother crossed the country with Tom, Chuck, and me, then moved to Rhode Island before Dad was shipped out. Then she lugged her three sons back to Wisconsin.

CHAPTER 4

Brother Tom, Our Yin and Yang:
A CONTEMPLATIVE LIFE, AN ACTIVIST LIFE

My younger brother Tom and I came at the world in different ways. In Jungian archetypes, he was the magician, I the warrior. Somehow, we stayed close through our lives. We were confidants, understanding each other better than anyone else. At 14 months apart, we were practically twins.

We had a lot in common. We were at the top of our classes in high school and college. We played pick-up sports every summer day and after school. In our teens, we hunted together in played-out cranberry bogs on the west shore of Green Bay, where Dad and his buddies leased an old farm and fishing port on the Little Suamico River. We bunked together there, two teenagers in sleeping bags in a barely heated old fishing shanty. We went to Bear Paw Boy Scout Camp together every summer in Mountain, Wisconsin. We both made Eagle Scout in Troop 6 run by Uncle John Walters. We made our family's annual hunting trip to Canada many times, from our teen years into our 70s, some years just the two of us.

We grew up skiing together on our local hill, Moon Valley Ski Club, in Green Bay. The love of the sport continued into our college years and beyond.

There was one bad ski day. Tom, a former high school racer who had made the Dartmouth ski team, and I were at Pico Peak in Vermont my senior year and his junior. Lured by an impending downhill race, we asked if we could run it. Dumb idea. We had quaffed a beer or two and hadn't checked out the slope. It had a giant catwalk across the fall line. We didn't know the course went around it. I just barely made it over the catwalk, finished and raced over to the official at the finish line so he could call up to the race start to stop Tom from running. It was too late. Never one to go slow, Tom hit the catwalk at a high speed, took a cartwheel and landed in a heap on its steep downside. I sprinted up the hill. He was only semi-conscious when I reached him.

I knew he was seriously hurt when I heard him moaning and muttering about his back. Two ski patrollers wanted to pick him up. Thankful now that we both made Eagle Scout, which included First Aid and Lifesaving, I vetoed the lift. I barked, "Don't move him!" I organized a six-man lift onto the toboggan. I held his back myself while we put sand bags around his legs and back and then took him down the mountain.

When we reached the bottom of the hill, the patrol started to take him off the toboggan to lift him into the ambulance. "Don't touch him," I ordered. We then lifted the entire toboggan with Tom still immobile into the ambulance. I rode to the Rutland Hospital by his side.

Diagnosis: three cracked vertebrae in his back. Movement could have paralyzed him. Recovering, he spent three-months in the Rutland, Vermont hospital. Soon he was partying with the nurses, lost a semester and went on a ten-year tear. After returning to school and continuing his party habits, he got a letter from the president of Dartmouth that read, "Dear Mr. Torinus, you have the distinction of recording the greatest grade point drop in the history of Dartmouth College."

He had already made Phi Beta Kappa in economics in his junior year, following Dad's footsteps. He later became a gifted writer and editor, the perfect guy to edit my master's thesis for the University of Stockholm on the Politics of the British Entry into

4. Brother Tom: Yin and Yang

the Common Market, later known as the European Union. He left a plum job as assistant general manager of the *New York Daily News* to visit me and edit my 90-page paper. It led to a first class degree. In addition to his editing, he dated most of the women in my circle of friends.

After Sweden, Dad lured Tom into the family business as a journalist and he became a very good one. As news director, he took Channel 11 in Green Bay from a dismal last place to number one in the market.

Tom liked zany stunts to snare viewers. One was to find out which Green Bay toilet paper manufacturer put out the longest roll. He lined them up in the Green Bay Packer football field and unrolled them for his viewers. I can't remember which company won to claim honors in the toilet paper capital of the world.

Later in life, he became a fine poet, earned master's degrees in psychology and divinity.

In 1987, I asked him to help me write a business plan to raise $28 million to buy Serigraph. He spent two weeks at my house in West Bend. Without investment bankers, he and I banged out a plan that got the deal done.

When Tom retired from the journalism business, he turned to a contemplative life and became a spiritual teacher and counselor. He served on my board at Serigraph for 20 years and was the first person I looked to for advice. I was always the action, go-do-it kind of guy; he was the yin to my yang.

He looked for deeper meaning while I opted for making things happen. We had a running dialogue about inner-directed and outer-directed life, realizing that each needs to be in a mix. It has been a creative tension that we became completely comfortable with in our later years.

Tom taught the executives at Serigraph the theory of Jungian archetypes, which postulates that we all have a mixture of Lover,

Warrior, Magician and King in our make-ups. My percentage on the Warrior side has always been high. That's OK. Different talents are needed in this world. Indeed, at Serigraph, we are always rearranging our management teams to achieve a balanced, optimum mix of talents and personality types.

Later on, Tom revealed that he had been very competitive with me in his early years, which was news to me. The first-born is looking ahead to figure things out, not to the rear. I was always just very proud of my brother and his gifts. Part of his perspective, of course, was my backside.

I feel the same pride about the rest of my siblings, with one exception. My youngest sister, Nancy, the fifth of six of us, married a man who saw the Torinus family as his enemy. She cut ties with all of us, including our mother.

Tom, brother Chuck, and I loved our youngest brother, Mark, as a brother and as a buddy. He was the life of the party for our family and we lost him way too early from a heart attack at 60. Like Tor, our father, Mark lived with more gusto than his body could handle over the long run.

One night while duck hunting in Saskatchewan, he fell flat on his face on the way to a shooting pass. He was immobile for a spell, then got up for the evening shoot. We later deduced that he had suffered a heart attack and his pace maker kicked in to save him. He made a couple of nice shots.

Tom and I have stayed close to the end of our days. We often celebrated our good fortunes, our loving family, and commiserated on our increasing number of ailments. We made a pact to talk every Sunday morning. As we entered our 80s, with the end in sight, Tom wrote these soothing words to me: "*From here in the front row, the view is infinite.*"

Our last joint project was to restore The Omelet, our family lodge, to its original stature. We had fun doing it.

4. Brother Tom: Yin and Yang

Tom signaled me in 2020 that he and his wife Mary were going to leave for eternity on their own terms. Both 82, Mary had severe and deteriorating dementia and Tom suffered very painful and worsening rheumatoid arthritis. Tom researched and discussed with Mary all dimensions of human departures, from medical to legal, ethical, and spiritual. They left for eternity painlessly in early 2021 — in bed, holding hands.

Brother Tom at a family wedding.

EDITORIAL POSTSCRIPT

Tom believed that we all have the right to live our lives as we choose and to end them on our own terms. All states should pass laws that allow dignified exits from the lives that only we own.

The Omelet — The Torinus family touchstone for generations.

Bertha (L) and V.I. Minahan built "The Omelet" in Egg Harbor in 1936 in the middle of the Great Depression.

CHAPTER 5

The Omelet, Our Family Touchstone
FIVE GENERATIONS OF PRECIOUS TIMES

Victor Ivan ("V.I.") Minahan, who built The Omelet in 1936 in the depths of the Great Depression, was a lawyer and a writer. It was he who painted it the color of a golden-brown omelet and named it as a word play on its location in Egg Harbor.

V.I. and his wife, Bertha Bush Torinus Minahan, often drove 70 miles on the dirt road from their home in De Pere to stay at the Alpine Resort in Egg Harbor. They grew to love Door County and decided to build a lodge-like place that could be a summer residence for them, their three children and grandchildren.

They picked a slight point south of the harbor on the choice lot in a new subdivision. It had 300 feet of frontage and privacy from the neighbors to the north and south because of the location on the tip of the gently curved point. Its hallmark was 900 feet of hand-crafted stonewall on the bay and road sides of the cottage. It must have taken thousands of man-hours to build that mortared wall with rocks pulled from the shore of the bay.

The architects for the project were Foeller, Schrober and Berners of Green Bay, according to blueprints dated Feb. 3, 1936.

The Omelet is strictly a summer place, built without insulation or basement. It has a great room, six bedrooms (one above the kitchen for the full-time maid), a kitchen and a small breakfast nook. The nook proved to be the most popular gathering spot even though it is the smallest space in the large cottage. Built to seat four, maybe six, it is not unusual for ten people to wedge

43

their way in for breakfast or conversations at other times of the day.

V.I. had the financial wherewithal to build the cottage, despite the Depression. He was a successful, practicing trial lawyer in Green Bay when he got the idea to start the *Free Press*, a daily publication that competed with the *Green Bay Gazette* in the 1920s. He later arranged a merger of the two publications into the *Green Bay Press-Gazette*. V.I. gave up law and became its editor and publisher. The newspaper, unlike other businesses, was a local unregulated monopoly and, therefore, somewhat impervious to the Depression.

During summers in his 60s and 70s, he and Bertha moved to the Omelet and he would use one of the first Dictaphones to record his editorials to a six-inch vinyl disc, which he would then mail to his secretary, Tracy Dugan, for transcription.

V.I. had been an artillery officer at the end of World War I, assigned to Battle Creek, Michigan, Bertha's hometown. She had returned home with her young son John after the early death of her first husband Burdette in 1915 in Stillwater, Minnesota. V.I. and Bertha met there, married and moved to Green Bay at the war's end. V.I. brought a wide range of knowledge and experiences to his insightful editorial writing.

His three children and five of his grandchildren became journalists and editorial writers.

He may not have foreseen that pattern or that the Omelet would become the family touchstone.

Its ownership transferred to John Torinus, Mary Walter and V.I. Jr., after V.I.'s death in 1953 and Bertha's passing in 1959. Dad later bought out his half-brother and half-sister, Vic and Mary, who subsequently bought their own places in Door County.

John and Louise Bambenek Torinus, their six children and 15 grandchildren spent as much time as they could at The Omelet.

5. The Omelet, Our Family Touchstone

The third generation got lots of invitations. "Tor" got into sailing on Green Bay and Lake Michigan and wrote two books about it. He was always looking for a crew to man his 33-foot Ranger sailboat called *Cheers*. We all became sailors.

In 1982, John and Louise transferred ownership to their six children and built a smaller place across the street, called "The Little One." It was a nifty solution to the commotion of active grandchildren playing in The Omelet's great room, from which there was little escape. The grandkids were still close by, but not too close.

Record high water in Lake Michigan in 1982 took out the stone plaza at the water's edge and the 300-foot wall along the shore of the property. The waves eroded half of the bayside lawn. It cost $40,000 to install a steel wall to prevent further erosion and to reclaim the front lawn. That barrier was far less elegant than the stone work it replaced, but there was little choice. The cottage itself was threatened. In some winters, huge piles of ice were thrown onto the lawn, almost to the structure itself.

Ironically, lake levels started to recede the following year and the waters of Green Bay never since touched the steel barrier. High water returned in 2019 but only splashes reached the steel. The lake dropped 17 inches in 2021.

Five of the six siblings owned The Omelet together for more than 30 years and it kept the family close. (Our estranged sister Nancy insisted on being bought out, even though our partnership agreement did not encompass a buyout.) We time-shared the summer weeks, pitched in with maintenance, put the long dock in every spring, took it out every fall and engaged in all manner of activities together.

It was Tom Torinus' concept to add a great porch to the bay side of the cottage. That addition in 2004, with Dan Sheehy as architect, proved to be a winner. The screened porch shifted some activity from the great room and protected guests on buggy days and evenings. And the porch added a touch of architectural distinction to an undistinguished structure.

The porch became the perfect place to watch the spectacular sunsets that have been the most treasured part of The Omelet experience. Visitors are advised to look for the "green flash" that occurs on the horizon just as the last sliver of the sun disappears at the end of another day. It is more often successfully observed after a martini or two.

Just as popular was Tom's addition of an open-air shower at the corner of the master bedroom overlooking Green Bay. It is a serene experience.

Mary Minahan Walter's marriage on the shore of Green Bay on the front lawn of The Omelet in 1937 was the first of ten family weddings there. It has also been the site of family reunions.

My marriage there to Caroline "Kine" Icks on June 11, 1994, was a lovely family affair. Wisconsin law enabled us to marry each other without an "officiant." So we wrote our own vows. Because we were both strong-minded, we included the First Amendment right to free speech in the exchange of vows. That was a little tongue-in-cheek. Tom Torinus presided at the ceremony and worked his word magic with his blessing of our union. Elizabeth "Abett" Icks, Kine's sister, did the same.

It was a second marriage for both of us and it was the beginning of many blessed years together. We were matched in all ways. We chose a spot for the ceremony under a birch tree on the north end of the bay shore lawn. A roiling storm rolled in from the southwest as the ceremony came to a hurried end.

Son Dan Torinus and Ingrid Klass also were married on the bayside lawn, choosing a spot on the south end of the property. They also matched well and got their marriage off to a fine start at

5. The Omelet, Our Family Touchstone

The Omelet. A storm also rolled in as their ceremony ended. They honeymooned at our cabin in northwest Wisconsin in Bayfield County on Little Bass Lake between Cable and Clam Lake.

In 2013, The Omelet went through another passage with the transfer of ownership to brothers John Torinus Jr. and Tom (80 and 20 percent, respectively) and their four children, the fourth generation to enjoy its charms. A fifth generation, the great-great-grandchildren of V.I. and Bertha, then took their turn at creating the commotion in the great room.

EDITORIAL POSTSCRIPT

The Omelet was our family touchstone for 85 years and it kept us in communication with each other through five generations. Ten family wedding were held on the bay shore. We owned it collectively many of those years, requiring frequent contact and working together. The "cottage" proved to be our super-glue.

As family members sold their shares and disconnected from The Omelet, we had to come up with new ways to stay close. Brother Tom and I came up with a simple but effective way to remain connected. We set up a weekly phone call with each other at 9 every Sunday morning.

Tom knew he was not long for this world and he wanted to make sure that in his last year, we stayed as bonded as we had been all our long lives. It worked wonderfully.

We talked about everything: our grandkids; the restoration of the Omelet, which we both worked on; old times, like hunting every year in Canada; skiing on small hills in Green Bay and later in the Alps; the aches and pains of us and our siblings; our former businesses; and all the good times we had along the way. Whatever came to our minds.

In a way, those regular conversations were Tom's nice way of saying goodbye to me.

They were reminiscent of Dad's daily letters to his wife Louise almost every day that he was away during World War II and later his weekly letters to his six children when they were away at college or in the service. We got carbon copies.

Tor was not openly affectionate one on one, the manly style in those days, but his letters let us know he loved us in a reliable, consistent way.

Taking a page from his book of life, I started weekly calls with my son Dan, who lives in the Madison area, with my brother Chuck in the Aspen area, and sister Laurie in Florida. We treasure being in close touch.

And we recommend regularity in family communications to all we know. Don't just drift apart.

CHAPTER 6

Hey, Diddle Diddle, Right Up the Middle:
ONLY BRUSHES WITH WAR

During an eight-week U.S. Marine Corps training exercise as a midshipman after my junior year at Yale, I proposed an envelopment maneuver (an end-around) to attack an enemy pill box.

"We don't do it that way," my drill instructor grunted. "In the Marines, we go *Hey, Diddle, Diddle, Right Up the Middle.*"

One squad or two of the three in a platoon would lay down a suppressing base of fire while the other squad advanced head-on, sometimes under return fire. With 50 yards gained, the squads would alternate and repeat until the objective was secured.

Lucky for me, I never had to use those tactics while I served three years on active duty as a lieutenant. There was a lull in armed combat during my tour of duty from 1959 to 1962.

Three years of service as an officer was a grand bargain in return for full tuition, room, board, books and expenses at Yale. I chose the Marine Corps option under the NROTC program instead of surface ships, submarines or jet planes, and it was a good fit. It was high privilege to be a Marine officer.

The Corps was natural for me. I had been around guns as a hunter since boyhood. Dad had been a lieutenant colonel in the Army, an imprint that was indelible. Boy scouting and hunting with Dad made me entirely comfortable in the outdoors.

The Marines gave young officers incredible responsibilities, but only after nine laborious months of training at Quantico, Virginia.

During boot camp, drill sergeants tried to put the fear of God into the newly minted lieutenants. One day we were signing a receipt for our paychecks (a paltry $225 per month) when a burly sergeant grabbed me by the shirtfront and put me up against the wall. I was almost six feet and weighed about 215 pounds. He screamed, "You dropped the pen on the table!" I was supposed to have passed it directly to the lieutenant behind me. I could hardly contain a smile at the theater of it. He must have been smiling on the inside, too.

If the mental harassment of officer boot camp didn't challenge college grads as hard as it did 18-year-old recruits, the physical part did. Many of the exercises were brutal, including carrying 60-pound packs on our backs for many miles. We ran tough obstacle courses. We competed running in boots on a seven -mile hill trail as a platoon. Everyone had to finish together, which meant dragging the slower, less physical members of the platoon across the finish line.

My buddy, Dick Tammaro, was not a runner. He weighed about 250 pounds. He crapped out on the top of the second of the seven hill climbs. I grabbed his weapon. Another guy grabbed his ammo; and my Yale buddy, Joe Staley, the toughest guy I have ever known, grabbed Dick and draped him over his shoulder. I held Dick up on the other side. We made the rest of the hills and crossed the finish line ahead of the other platoons. It was just a training exercise, nowhere near real war.

Dick joined the FBI after discharge and we remained friends all our lives. He organized the 50th reunion of our officers group and spouses in 2012 in Newport Beach, Rhode Island. It was like we had never been apart. Dick, Roger Williams, Don Kempf and I with our wives talked for hours about the Corps and lives led.

Sick of schooling when the nine months of training ended, we were assigned to active duty. I drew artillery, the 11th Marine

6. Hey, Diddle, Diddle, Right Up the Middle

Best buddies, three Marine lieutenants: me, Don Kempf, and David Henderson, my scuba partner, who died during a training exercise at Camp Pendleton, California.

After discharge from the Corps in 1962, I headed home to Wisconsn in my TR3 with all my earthly possessions, including my scuba gear.

Mom and me in uniform, Christmas ball,1961. She was a beautiful dancer, light as a ballerina.

6. Hey, Diddle, Diddle, Right Up the Middle

Regiment in the 1st Marine Division at Camp Pendleton, California. It was a proven outfit, with a long, distinguished record.

I had gotten to know Roger Williams at Quantico and we linked up at Oceanside. We schemed to report only when the BOQ (bachelor officers' quarters) was full. That nifty maneuver allowed us to find a residence off base. Seven poorly paid lieutenants pooled our funds to rent a place called "The Storybook House," right on a fabulous beach on the south side of Oceanside.

We worked our butts off while on duty, but our off hours were a hoot. Dave Henderson got me into scuba diving. That meant a steady supply of lobster and abalone. On the down side, there were precious few young women around the Marine base. I was getting tired of all-male institutions.

Adding to our larder of seafood, I shot a deer on the base with an M1. We butchered it on the linoleum floor in the kitchen, following step-by-step directions from the classic cookbook given to me—*The Joy of Cooking*.

The guys had big appetites and I was elected cook for the group. My masterpiece was a 25-pound meatloaf derived from Grandma Bambenek's recipe (oatmeal, spices, raw eggs mixed with pork, veal, and beef). It lasted two days. We were poor, but ate well.

I still can't believe how fast the Corps moved us along. We all started out as forward observers (FO), the dubious assignment of being ahead of friendly lines to direct our 105-millimeter howitzer to selected targets. Because of my exposure to engineering, I was assigned to the S-3 operations office, which ran the Fire Direction Center. It received input from the FOs and aerial observers to pinpoint targets. It was a technology center, revolving around ballistics. I ended up as S-3 running the Center, a major's billet. Our biggest exercise, again far short of real war, was "TOT" — a time on target where five batteries and a battle-ship all put their massive rounds on the same target — from far different firing points — landing simultaneously. It worked, to my amazement.

On a not-so-good day, one of my lance corporals made a 1000-mil subtraction error on a 3600-mil protractor (no comput-ers back then). One battery, therefore, was 90 degrees off target, and the rounds dropped near our truck park. Artillery is dangerous business. No people or trucks were hurt. Had there been an unluckier outcome, I could have been court-martialed as the officer in charge.

CLOSE TO WAR TWICE

I came close to war two times. On October 27 and 28, 1961, President Kennedy and Soviet Premier Nikita Khrushchev had tanks squared off after the Soviets and East Germans had built the 2.5-mile wall separating East and West Berlin over the previous summer. It was a dangerous game of chicken, engendered by the flood of East Germans escaping to the West via Berlin.

Both sides put their troops on alert. Our California regiment mounted up. We signed our wills, put our dog tags around our necks, packed our howitzers and waited at the air strip at El Toro Marine Base — ready to go. We were on the landing strip for 48 hours before Kennedy and Khrushchev cut a deal to turn off tensions. The tanks backed off. Neither side wanted war over the wall. We were relieved when our unit returned to Camp Pendleton.

The wall stayed in place all during the Cold War. Families were tragically separated. Escapees died as they tried numerous ways to get out. The would climb over or tunnel under the wall or swim across a channel watched by heavily armed guards.

6. Hey, Diddle, Diddle, Right Up the Middle

Flash forward. In 1991, I went to Berlin on business and crossed Check Point Charlie, the controlled, guarded passage through the remains of the wall, into a grim, gray, depressed East Berlin, as part of *Glasnost* under Russian leader Mikhail Gorbachev, the wall was abandoned. I watched as Germans from both sides and foreigners tore the wall down, brick by brick, piece by piece. Traffic between the two Germanies reopened in late 1989. By 1992, the wall was gone. Its bricks were relics.

In a span of 30 years in my life, I was witness to both the erection and dismantling of the Berlin Wall.

In my last months in the Corps, I took over as commander of the Headquarters Company of the 2nd battalion. It was a privilege to have 200 Marines directly under my command.

In my other brush with real war, I was assigned to a top-secret project in early 1962. I had been trained in artillery nuclear weapons (a Dr. Strangelove, I was) and had top-secret clearance. I was assigned to ballistics and logistics work behind a barbed wire enclosure at Pendleton. I thought I was planning an amphibious operation into Vietnam, where "the conflict" was heating up in early 1962. My guess was off target.

I had made the wrenching decision to leave military service as my tour of duty came to a close in early 1962 and mustered out in June. That fall, while visiting my former commanding officer, Lt. Col. Cal Kileen, who had become military attaché to Denmark, I learned that the whole 1st Marine Division had mounted up, moved through the Panama Canal and was sitting off Cuba as the Soviet nuclear missiles made their way south on the Atlantic in October 1962. It was another Kennedy-Khrushchev standoff, this time much more serious, close to World War III. Unbeknownst to me, I had been part of the planning team for an invasion of Cuba.

55

Straight Talk From the Heartland

My discharge in June 1962 was a sad parting. I was losing contact with best friends and a service I loved. I sent a trunk of uniforms home and loaded up the sum total of the rest of my belongings in my TR3 sports car (black with red leather seats), including my scuba gear, Hawaiian sling and skis strapped on top, and headed home to De Pere, Wisconsin.

Even though I had decided on Europe for grad school, I still had a five-year obligation remaining in the USMC Reserves. The ill-conceived Vietnam War started heating up in 1964 and I was expecting a call-up. It never happened. Marine regulars volunteered for repeated tours, so the reserves were never needed. Vietnam was a nasty, unwinnable guerilla war. I was lucky to have missed it. (In later conflicts, the reservists often were routinely called up.)

The Marine experience was indelible. I never stopped thinking of myself as a jarhead. I had seriously considered a career in the Corps, but a wider world called.

I learned a ton in the Corps that has stayed with me all my life:

- Rigorous, respectful leadership matters; the world needs all kinds of people. It really needs individuals who are not afraid to step forward and lead when necessary.

- *Esprit de corps* starts at the top with a compelling mission and honorable leaders.

- Purposefulness (*"We will take that hill."*) must be part of a leader's DNA. Failure is not an option.

- Some pomp and circumstance, like parades and ceremonies, need to be part of the fabric of life and organizations.

- Humans are capable of much more challenge than they think.

- The troops eat first, then the officers.

6. Hey, Diddle, Diddle, Right Up the Middle

I did don my uniform one more time — on November 10, 2015. I was invited to an annual Marine Ball in Wisconsin and was sure my old blues uniform would fit. I was 20 pounds lighter at 78 than I had been at 24. To my embarrassment, I couldn't button the tight-fitting jacket. My wife Kine, daughter of a Marine hero, laughed lovingly and said, "Everything has sunk a bit." I had to hire a seamstress to let out the pants and jacket an inch. I love those dress blues with the red stripe down the pant leg.

I was accompanied to the ball by Kine. Her dad, Karl Icks, fought at 17 at the Battle of Belleau Wood outside Paris in World War I. His regiment stopped the German advance 60 miles outside of Paris, and the Marines were labelled "the devil dogs" by the Germans. That battle in June 1918 triggered the end of the war. It also established the Corps as a front-line, elite fighting force.

Kine and I had a ball at the ball. I felt a little under-dressed as the only Marine without battle ribbons.

EDITORIAL POSTSCRIPT

Every young person in America should have the opportunity for a full, paid-for education, like I enjoyed. But not a free education. The payback could be several years of national service, like I did. That second part was just as educational as the first. It was a fair deal for me and for the country. "Free education" is a bad bargain.

Above, coat of arms of Stockholm, Sweden; below, logo of the University of Stockholm

CHAPTER 7

Ja Tala Litta Svenska:
(I TALK A LITTLE SWEDISH)

My path became clear when I decided not to make a career of the Marine Corps. Life in the corps was good stuff. I loved all of it, from the rigor, the proud tradition to the red stripe. But, at the level of junior officer, life was pretty narrow and confining. There were lots of rules and regs and not much space for creativity or carving your own way. The Corps is hierarchical, at least until younger officers are on the front lines, where they are mostly on their own, and it has to be that way. Marines are not innovators; they are warriors. It's a different deal.

My path was supposed to be business — specifically the Harvard Business School where I had been accepted into its renowned MBA program. But that program was then all male and I had endured enough of that: St. Norbert's (all male), Yale (all male), the Corps (all male). I didn't look forward to another high testosterone, ultra-competitive, grind-it-out male establishment.

By then I had decided to become a journalist, in particular a foreign correspondent. My dad had lured me in that direction by asking that I write editorials on foreign and military policy while serving in the Corps. He published them, and I was hooked.

There was an alternative to Harvard. During my summer NROTC cruise on the battleship *Iowa* between my junior and senior years in 1958, we stopped in Copenhagen and Guantanamo Bay, Cuba. I remember it being 120 degrees in the engine room in Cuba and loading 50-pound bags of powder into the chambers of the *Iowa*'s 16-inch guns during firing exercises. We slept in racks stacked five deep, with just enough clearance to roll over. There were 3000 men on that amazing war machine. We were supposed to get a three-day pass to Havana, but the Castro revolution was heating up and our passes were revoked. We were confined to the Gitmo naval base.

Our layover in Copenhagen was another story. The Tivoli Gardens were magical for a young man. That central park and amusement center shimmered with white lights that outlined trees, restaurants, taverns and konditoris. It was summer, but it was like Christmas in Wisconsin and it was full of beautiful girls.

I had read about Scandinavia being the "land of free love," and I believed it, as if love ever were.

I checked out the University of Copenhagen and it had a one-year English-speaking program. Unfortunately, it had been discontinued, but the University of Stockholm had a similar program, to which I was referred. I accepted its offer and turned down prestigious Harvard.

It was a fork in the road and only infrequently did I think I might have chosen the wrong one. Had I taken the other road, I probably would have become a freakin' investment banker on Wall Street, the shallowest existence one could conjure up. Those guys do abstract transactions, the exact opposite of a real life dealing with real people, real products, real outcomes. So, no regrets, despite the mega-millions the soulless Wall Street middlemen extract from the capitalist system.

I spent a lot of time learning about Sweden's "Middle Way," a middle path between capitalism and socialism. In 1963, it was a homogenous country, where there was an overriding consensus in favor of social welfare. It still is for the most part, but has swung back to free markets after years of tepid growth. Marginal taxes were then 90 percent, part of its egalitarian polity and economy.

While essentially capitalistic and very democratic, Sweden struck me as an unexciting society and the Swedes liked it that way. It's a quiet place, a refined place, a disengaged, neutral place. Everyone was very polite.

It lacked the robustness, the go-for-it, individualistic character of my home country.

I also had a hard time with Sweden's neutrality in World War II, though it saved the country from war's ravages. Sweden's white flag made for compromises with the Nazis, with the West and with the Jews. For the most part, they were very pragmatic about it all. They preferred the sidelines as Hitler perpetrated atrocities to the front lines.

The best part of my sojourn to Sweden was the company of my fellow graduate students from all over the world. The Nigerians taught me to dance with abandon. Doing the *La Bamba* late one night with a little too much abandon, I tore my hamstring and spent three months in a cast. The foreign students partied with Swedish friends on dreamy mid-summer nights. The birds would be singing in the sunrise light when we headed home at 3 a.m. Hunter Mayboon, my Scottish shot-put friend who spoke six languages, punched out a nice Swedish fellow, a student leader, who tried to quiet one of our parties in the dorm. He called his form of diplomacy "The Big Right." Brian Linklater, a Canadian trumpet player, was my study buddy. A black American guy learned the Swedish language in several months because he jabbered away without inhibitions, not worrying about being perfect.

November 22, 1963, of course, stands out for everyone of my vintage. I was in the student union that evening, mingling with some Swedish and international friends, hanging out. The news ricocheted through the union that John F. Kennedy, the dashing, young American president, had been assassinated in Dallas,

Texas. JFK had won the hearts of Europeans and that included the Swedes. They would have elected him president of their country. We were all shocked and angry. My Swedish friends were as saddened as we Americans. In retrospect, he was a visionary, but a reckless and undisciplined president who nearly got us into World War III. But he charmed the world.

Brother Tom came over to visit me on a lark, ostensibly to edit my thesis. He had recently left a big job at the *New York Daily News* to carve his own way. First stop: Stockholm.

My sojourn to Sweden also started out as a bit of a lark, the end product being a one-year certificate, but my serious side won out. I decided to stay on for a master's degree in international relations, a combination of political science and economics. Nils Andreen, a political scientist, was my professor and mentor. I liked him a lot, partly because he left neutral Sweden during the war to work for British intelligence. That set him apart.

There were not a lot of classes in Swedish graduate school, but there was a ton of reading and a major thesis involved. Andreen steered me into taking a hard look at the politics of the pending entry by the United Kingdom into what was then called the Common Market. I put enormous effort into that project, including a summer doing interviews with political leaders in London and research at the London School of Economics. Roy Wilson, the head of the British Labour Party in the early 1960s, was one of my interviewees. He became Prime Minister in 1964.

Britain did enter the EU in 1974, but not all the way, reflecting the ambivalence and division in its population in the 1960s about staying an independent island or joining the continent. The Brits kept the pound as their currency and never adopted the Euro, one of the key elements of belonging to the union.

Flash forward 50 years, and the Brits were still conflicted about being part of the Common Market, later renamed the

European Union (EU). Polls in 2014, a half-century later, showed momentum toward a "Brexit," a secession. A referendum was called for 2016 on whether to stay or go. I had bet that the Brits would decide to stay allied, but to separate. England had figured out how to adapt to global markets and fiscal constraint, while the social welfare states on the continent remained mired in government subsidies, inertia and sluggish growth. The "Brexit" rejection of the EU in 2017 came as a surprise to those who didn't know of the United Kingdom's unenthusiastic embrace back in the late 1960s and early 1970s.

During the summer of 1963, I found a flat above the "Hero of Maida Pub" on Edgeware Road and put on 20 pounds drinking ale with the chaps who hung out there, including novelist Kingsley Amis. It was a great summer. Brian Linklater and I had a lively time taking on some of the accomplished street debaters at Hyde Park.

Back in Sweden, I defended my thesis in front of a panel of professors and won a First Class Degree. Tom's editing made the difference.

Here are the first and third paragraphs of my thesis in 1964 on the confusion of the two British political parties on whether to join what was then called the "Common Market."

"During the course of the Great Debate over the proposed British entry into the European Economic Community (EEC), it became part of the political jargon to describe the Labor Party's position as 'sitting on the fence.'"

"Political analysts also made cases that the Conservative Party had never wholly abandoned the fence either, even though Prime Minister Macmillan seemed to have taken cautious steps in the direction of Europe."

Flash forward 55 years and the Brits were still split right down the middle on staying or exiting the European Union.

Nothing ever got that controversial in Sweden. There was much to like about the relative harmony and homogeneity of the Swedish political system in the 1960s. The monarchy had long been largely ceremonial, perched on top of a parliamentary system. The most impressive piece of its "Middle Way" was the collaboration between the private sector, political leaders and the government.

Every bill went through a "remiss" system in which all major interests weighed in before passage. Most were consensus bills before they became law. It is governance almost totally opposite to the fractious, hyper-partisanship of the U.S. system in the 2000s. Or, should I say, dysfunctional non-system? Partisanship had all but destroyed the U.S. political center by the presidential campaign of 2016. Trump's four years in office were a disaster for our democracy. In addition to being an anti-moral human being, he was a train wreck for disciplined government. He would have never won anything in Sweden.

Swedish welfare spending was high; military spending was moderate; the education systems were among the best in the world; the state owned a monopoly in liquor sales, which were robust. Every young Swedish man had to serve time in the military reserves.

Life was pleasant there. Yet, I thoroughly missed the dynamism that comes with living in the country at the center of the action in the world. America has its issues, but it is a creative, pulsing place. I was ready to get back to America and get on with life.

My lovely girlfriend Margareta, a blond artist, had no interest in moving to America, and, who can blame her? Sweden is a nice place. So that was the end of that. I often wondered how her life played out.

When it was time to go home, Tom and I were almost broke. We had about $400 between us. We booked second-class tickets on the Ventura, a third-rate passenger ship out of Barcelona. Then, Tom's suitcase, with his wallet inside, was stolen, so now we were really broke. Second Class was deep in the hold of the ship and full of Italian immigrants heading to the U. S. Nice people, but it was crowded and stinky. We couldn't afford drinks, so we drank the cheap second-class table wine.

With pluck and luck, we parlayed our way to First Class during the day by offering to play bridge with some elderly ladies. They invited us to the upper deck every day.

After a seven-day trip, it was uplifting to see the Statue of Liberty greeting us after two years abroad.

Editorial Postscript

The country and Wisconsin could benefit greatly from the consensus-building methods Sweden deploys on complex policy issues. The partisan warfare here tears a country apart. The partisan warriors, often lobbyists, love the combat. That's how they make their livings. The Wisconsin Idea, which long encouraged collaborative politics, died under governors Doyle, Walker, and Evers. Can it be brought back?

The ᴅᵃⁱˡʸWest Bend News

VOL. 116, NO. 1   Official Newspaper of Washington County   West Bend, Wis. 53095, Monday, Oct. 5, 1970   16 Pages, Two Sections   PRICE 10 CENTS

At One A.M. Today, The News Became a Daily Paper

DAILY NEWS

A Trusted News Source Since 1855

SATURDAY MORNING APRIL 1, 1995   ★ ★ THE LAST EDITION

April 1st, 1995 marked the last publication of the *Milwaukee Sentinel*. I had left that wonderful paper in 1987. It merged into the *Milwaukee Journal Sentinel*.

CHAPTER 8

Have Newsman's Trench Coat, Will Travel:
EVERLASTING FUN IN THE NEWSROOM

I had no intention of going into my father's newspaper world when I got out of college. I was recruited in my senior year at Yale to take a job at Proctor & Gamble (P&G) at its newly acquired Charmin toilet paper mill in Green Bay. The term "pre-job" applies, because I only worked there a couple weeks before reporting for military duty. The idea was to accrue three years of seniority while in the service and then start a career after three years of active duty. In that short stint, the mill manager asked me to map all the sewer and water lines and electrical conduits in the massive plant on the East River. "Is that what engineers do?" I asked myself. I pretty much decided then and there that I would not be going back.

For whatever reason, I had no ambition for climbing a big corporate ladder. My parents never pushed me in that — or any — direction. I wanted an interesting life. In retrospect, bailing out of Charmin might have been a mistake, because it was P&G's initial move into consumables in personal hygiene. I would have been in on the ground floor of what would become a huge global division.

So, instead of going the direction of my manufacturing grandfather, D.C. Bambenek, I headed to toward the newspaper-ing world of my father and step-grandfather, V. I. Minahan. How did that happen in a world of many options? I guess, like lots of young people, I gravitated to the familiar.

I didn't know much about the news business, beyond what I had picked up by osmosis from the family, but figured I had the makings of a foreign correspondent with my military chops and degree in international relations. Somewhat prematurely, I bought the uniform of the profession, a trench coat, then headed off to UW–Madison for summer school for a minor on how to do news.

I took six courses and learned to write obits and leads. Madison summer school is famous for its partying. I was still a dork and even though the coeds were lovely, I couldn't figure out how to engage. I really did need to get the basics of my chosen profession under my belt.

While there, I sent out 50 resumes and applications to leading newspapers; most did not respond. But two did, even though I had zero experience. One was the distinguished Minneapolis Tribune, the morning paper in a very dynamic metro area. I jumped at the chance, got hired and was on my way. Footnote: I never wore the trench coat on an assignment.

The editors like to keep cub reporters humble. Egos get pumped up when you see your byline in the paper. My first came when I was assigned to interview Arthur Godfrey, the national radio show host. I did as told and produced a six-inch story. His star was on the wane and he had just fired his long-time lead singer, Julius LaRosa ("When the moon hits your eye like a big pizza pie . . . ."). So I asked him about LaRosa. "He was a schmuck," said Godfrey. I turned in the story with that quote. Stu Baird, city editor, bellowed across the newsroom — I was seated way back at the last desk — "Torinus, do you know what a 'schmuck' is?" I tried to be inconspicuous. "It's Yiddish for penis," he yelled and cackled. The newsroom thought it was hilarious. I deleted the quote in the rewrite.

Working in the newsroom of a morning metro paper was a hoot, all day, every day, except for the obituaries assigned to all new reporters. They had to be letter and grammar perfect. (I still do obits for family and friends.)

The newsroom held a menagerie of characters. There was classy Barbara Flanigan, the society editor, as they were called then, who once wrote a festive holiday season headline: "Balls, Balls, Balls." Sports columnist Jim Klobuchar showed me how to race from the newsroom after the 11 p.m. deadline for the last of four editions to a nearby saloon and get down a couple of martinis before closing. Jane Brody, like me a cub reporter, who went on to become a star writer for the *New York Times* and author, could always get a story out of the cops on the crime beat when I couldn't. Jane was smart, lively and buxom.

A couple of the worn-out newsmen on the horseshoe copy desk had cigarettes hanging from the sides of their mouths, ashes on their lapels and one had a flask in a brown paper bag in his inside breast pocket. They delighted in finding mistakes in copy, especially when the reporters chafed at the critique. I loved it all.

Those were the glory days of newspapering. We were still using typewriters, the machine invented in Milwaukee, and cheap copy paper. You would yank your last page out of the typewriter and yell: "Copy boy," and an intern would run your story to the copy editors. On deadline, they would grab it one page at a time. The copy perfectionists used thick black pencils to chop up our prose. You got quick, sharp feedback from the black corrections. From them, the story would go to the city desk, where another round of editors would go over it for content. Finally, it was jammed on a 10-inch spike, waiting to move to the linotype operators, where they turned words into lead type at three lines a minute.

That elaborate process gave way to computerized typesetting within a decade. Gone were the copy desk curmudgeons and their black pencils. The end of their feedback to reporters was a loss.

My rookie experience would have been less stressful had I learned to type. That deficit got me transferred off the fast-moving rewrite desk in short order. I preferred reporting any way. (Like my dad, I never learned to type with more than four fingers on one hand and two on the other.)

As a general reporter, I covered tornadoes, a flood, murders and other mayhem on Hennepin Avenue in downtown Minneapolis, civil rights protests, and even reviewed a few theatrical performances. One tornado in suburban Anoka had flattened 400 homes by the time I got there. While assessing the damage, a second twister hit and I dived for cover in a culvert. I phoned in a first-person story.

Covering a flood of the Mississippi River that topped its banks in St. Paul, I saw a head bobbing above the turbulent current. A good swimmer, I started to wade in but the head disappeared. I wisely retreated from the roiling waters and later learned that the guy had jumped from a bridge.

The most colorful murder I covered, amidst a bunch of ordinary murders, was that of a teenaged babysitter who was grabbed from a home in St. Paul. Neighbors heard the sounds of screeching tires about the time of the abduction. Several days later, while covering a national governor's convention in Minneapolis, the call came about 10 o'clock from the city desk assigning me to follow up on a tip that the girl's body had been found.

I grabbed a company car and a photographer. We headed into the night to a remote area north of St. Paul. We were driving around about midnight when we ran into a deputy sheriff who directed us to a town dirt road. His tip wasn't much help, because we saw no one, and it was very dark. We drove and drove. I finally told the photographer to turn around and head back. He got stuck in loose sand on the shoulder. I had to get out and push the car. We drove about a quarter of a mile when it dawned on me: I had been standing on the loose sand of the emptied grave. We rushed back; I smoothed out the sand, and he got a shot. It appeared in the next morning's paper with a white outline around the temporary grave. We had a scoop on the two St. Paul papers and our sister paper, the afternoon Minneapolis Star.

It got better. I went back the next morning for a second-day story and saw the reporters from the other papers finally on the scene, trying to catch up. Brilliantly, if I may say, I started peering down an old well and had our photographer take a shot. The other photographers did, too. They ran that shot on their front pages — a grave site that never was. Gotcha. It might have been juvenile, but it sure was fun. It later turned out that the killer actually had used the well as interim storage before moving her body to the sandy grave. The killer was sentenced to life in a mental hospital.

The newsroom managers decided that I was best suited for the business beat. That started my career as a business and economics journalist. It was a good fit.

After a little more than a year at the *Tribune*, my dad made an offer to join the family newspapers in Wisconsin as an editor. City editor of the *Tribune,* Stu Baird, who had taken a chance on me, was really upset. I never felt quite right about leaving the *Tribune* after only 13 months, an apprenticeship where I got far more than I gave.

It might have been a major mistake. Family businesses, as I learned later many times over, can be tricky. I thought that I could work my way up to the publisher position in the family corporation.

Dad knew I liked challenges and had a bent for management. He offered me the opportunity to fix a major Post Corporation screw-up. In their wisdom, my father and uncle, V.I. Jr., both Phi Beta Kappas, (Dartmouth and Stanford), decorated officers in

World War II, listened to the numbers guy in the executive ranks, David Nelson, a Rasputin in our public but family-controlled company. They followed his hard-nosed lead and decided in 1964 to "force" the sale of a new Sunday edition of the *Appleton Post-Crescent*. It had been a six-day paper, and they told their subscribers they had no option but to take the new Sunday publication in a seven-day subscription. They overlooked that customers almost always have options. They could drop the paper or they could switch to a competitor. In the Twin Cities of Neenah and Menasha to the south of Appleton in the Fox River Valley, the reaction to the "force" was fierce. Circulation dropped from 11,000 to about 7,000, many switching to the six-day *Oshkosh Daily Northwestern*, a competitor to the south.

It became my job to get the lost subscribers back.

Nelson had no feel for people or markets. He was a tough guy, a numbers guy, a bully really. My dad and uncle were nice guys, too nice. They went along with his heavy-handed decision to force seven days of payments. In business, bullies abound, but save me from nice guys, too. By that I mean executives who won't make the hard calls, who won't confront the bullies. Dad and Vic learned the hard way that they should have tested the market deeply before the Sunday launch. They hadn't shown enough respect for their customers. They did no focus groups or surveys. They could have used carrots, incentives, to move up to a seven-day paper, instead of the big stick. They should have trusted their nice guy natures.

But, hey, we all make bad calls. The only people who don't make mistakes are the ones on the sidelines. The damage was done. Further, Dad, the editor and general manager, and Vic, the publisher, put out a fine newspaper, far better than the Northwestern. Their recovery concept was brilliant. Together in 1965, we created a small daily for Neenah-Menasha that went inside the parent daily, the *Post-Crescent*. The piggyback daily, a former weekly, was called the *Twin City News-Record*. It was the second of four daily editions of the *Post-Crescent*. It developed a life of its own for those two cities and the rest of Winnebago County.

Neenah and Menasha had always been an odd couple community. Menasha was largely a blue-collar city, home to union workers in the local paper mills. Neenah was where the papermaking executives lived in large mansions on the Fox River or the shores of Lake Winnebago. Neenah had the reputation of having the highest per capita income in the United States, right up there with Scarsdale, New York.

The vertical drop of the Fox River from Neenah to Green Bay, one of the few north flowing rivers in the country, is 168 feet. Its swift current enabled hydroelectric power, which powered several dozen paper mills along the river. Those mills made the Fox River Valley the center of the paper industry for a century. The Twin Cities (of Neenah/Menasha), the first stop on the north-flowing river, were a prosperous place.

I knew that I would need a news team that was first rate. My star recruits were Peter Geniesse, a Notre Dame grad who went on to edit our Sunday newspaper and write several books on the plight of Hispanic immigrants to the U.S., legal and illegal; Cliff Miller, a UW-Madison grad who went on to head our Capitol bureau; George Mancoskey, our sports editor who knew every kid who ever played anything in the Twin Cities. I wrote a daily editorial.

My best management tool was a daily mark-up of our newspaper after it hit the streets. I posted it in the newsroom, where red ink showed where we had beaten the Northwestern crew or vice versa and where we could improve going forward. Our "scoops" far out-weighed theirs, and we brought back the lost subscribers.

For a small community, it was crazy competition. I remember when Rollie Kampo, Town of Menasha chairman, called a press conference. Six competing reporters and journalists showed up. A town chairman calling a press conference? When had that ever happened before or since? It was about an important subject: Kampo's town was fighting the annexation by the City of Menasha of the Banta Company, a sizeable book printer. The case went to the Wisconsin Supreme Court, where the city won in a 4-3 decision. Kampo was a smart, redneck character, and the city attorney was Richard Steffens, a short, cigar-smoking, bow-tied, tough-talking lawyer. Both were colorful and they made for great copy. I got to know both well.

Our formula for success was local news, local news, local news. No matter how much we published, our readership surveys showed us that our readers wanted even more.

It took us about two years to get the Neenah-Menasha circulation back to the pre-"force" level of 11,000.

What I remember most was the pure pleasure of working with a team of professionals. It was much like the camaraderie that I had experienced in my company in the Marine Corps. We worked very hard, including long hours covering seemingly interminable night meetings: school boards, planning commissions, city councils and their committees, even library boards. We covered the community like a down-filled blanket. We published bowling scores, honor rolls, births, long obituaries that often made front page and most of the police blotter. We dug out story after story that the Northwestern never got.

Our staff also played and partied together. We became life-long friends. We stood up in each other's weddings. It was the best of times.

8. Have Newsman's Trench Coat, Will Travel

Those years were some of my happiest because I met and married Pati Platten, a beautiful, athletic, highly intelligent woman from Green Bay. We were soul mates for many years.

ANOTHER DAILY NEWSPAPER; ANOTHER CHAPTER

After a year's sabbatical for a Congressional Fellowship in Washington D.C., my dad and uncle challenged me again. I could have stayed in the world of big-time politics with Donald Rumsfeld, who was in the first Nixon cabinet in 1969, but I was always a deeply rooted Wisconsin guy. It was their challenge to create a daily newspaper in West Bend, Wisconsin, that brought me back.

It would become the 36th daily paper in the state — probably the last, as we learned later, ever to be created in the U.S. That was still the heyday of print newspapering. Community dailies were virtual monopolies on a small scale and they made a ton of money. Publishers and general managers thought they were superstars as they brought home pre-tax profits in the 30 to 40 percent range. In retrospect, they were easy businesses to run.

Because they were so profitable, chains started to aggregate local newspaper properties. They were willing to pay 40 times earnings, or four times sales volume, because the cash flows were enormous. The second and third generation publishers, the guys who were born on third base, were more than happy to sell out at those multiples and then hit the beach for life.

The Internet was just a concept back then, so I doubt if the sellers were clairvoyant and foresaw the web-based threat to the print media that would arrive with a vengeance 20 years later. I certainly didn't see the massive disruption ahead. Internet news was to become one of the most disruptive technologies ever in business history. By the turn of the century, large daily newspapers were in trouble all over the country. By 2015, more than half of U.S. adults were getting most of their news from web-based social media. Newspaper circulation had fallen by one-half and their advertising revenues followed suit.

My wife Pati and I arrived in West Bend in early October 1969, just two weeks after the birth of our first son, Sean (John Bush Torinus III). We were nearly broke after a year on meager Fellow's pay. We drove our old Dodge Aspen station wagon home from D.C. with a U-Haul trailer and all our possessions in tow. We found a small rental house on 10th Street for $125 a month. It was a block from the city's Regner Park, a WPA project from the 1930s that featured a large swimming lagoon, a baseball diamond and tennis courts. We made a lot of new friends our age, mainly through tennis and were happy. I loved being a father to a wonderful son.

I must have taken the assignment of creating a daily seriously. I thought I was impervious to stress, having run a high-stress fire direction center in the Marine Corps, having started another daily and just off media fire-fighting for Donald Rumsfeld as he ran the controversial federal anti-poverty program. I wasn't impervious. To my utter surprise, the stress got to me in very physical ways. I developed a skin rash over the middle half of my body, a tick in my left eye, and hemorrhoids. I was 32 and very mortal. No longer cocky about my workaholic tendencies, I tried to back off. Lesson learned.

The formula that had worked in Neenah-Menasha also worked in West Bend: great team work, this time with a crew of veteran newsmen; intense coverage of local news, from bowling scores to dispatches from Madison from Cliff Miller that affected Washington County; and full engagement of the community.

8. Have Newsman's Trench Coat, Will Travel

Being an editor of a local newspaper is like being a country doctor. You get to know the people in the community close up and personal. You are the court of last resort. When people are frustrated with local officials and have struck out trying to get answers, they call the editor. Sometimes coverage of their issues yields positive outcomes. At least, they get heard.

I wrote a column three times a week, abandoning the impersonal, institutional editorials that had been part of the industry forever. The personal touch proved far more effective in connecting with readers.

The Huber family, which had owned the weekly before Post Corp. acquired it, had vetoed political coverage of the Democratic Party — Democrats were given no space by Mama Huber. Though retired, she let me know she was not happy with my change to an even-handed approach. Local Democrats were, of course, delighted with the change of direction. Washington County had always been bedrock for the GOP, but the local manufacturing companies were mostly unionized and there were plenty of Democrats to sign up as subscribers. The local Republicans really expected no more than equal coverage.

Unfortunately, Mark Huber died suddenly at age 42, about six months after I arrived. He had stayed on as general manager after his family sold out. He was a fine, smart man, with a physics degree from St. Norbert College. We worked well together. I had to assume the added role of general manager, helped by my exposure to engineering at Yale and management in the Marines.

While the Internet had not yet arrived, Mark had installed two photo-electronic typesetters, among the first to hit the market. It was sad to see the linotype machines and their lead type become history. We had to retrain the grizzled old linotypers to use the new gear. They had used three fingers on the linotype keyboard, which allowed them to hold a cigarette between their two outside fingers. We saved major labor dollars as we went from seven lines of type a minute to 25.

It was a first step toward reporters setting the type with their original keystrokes and the elimination of typesetters altogether. It was a harbinger of fully digitized graphics and page make-up on computer screens.

Our only real competition came from *The Milwaukee Journal*, the powerhouse afternoon metro daily and the *Milwaukee Sentinel*, the scrappy morning Hearst-owned daily. Neither paid much real attention to the exurban areas like Washington County. Even though the *Journal* had a suburban bureau, we had a lot of running room.

There was a new form of competition for local advertising dollars in the form of "shopper" publications. They carried little, if any, news and were distributed free, usually once a week to 100 percent of the homes in the market. That compared to about 50 percent penetration by newspapers. Mark Huber had created a shopper, called *The Post*, to fend off entrants to our market of about 30,000 homes. I moved *The Post* to Sunday, so we had seven-day coverage for advertisers. Then I added a second one, called *The Advantage*, a mid-week shopper that went only to homes not covered by *The Daily News*. We used many combinations of cross-selling ad rates to give retailers whatever impact they wanted during the week. We owned the market.

The *West Bend Daily News* and its sister shoppers were a roaring success. From a base of 9,000 subscribers, we grew quickly. I bought billboard space to run just one big number every time we added another thousand homes: 10,000, 11,000, 12000, 13,000 and finally a plateau of 14,000. That campaign gave *The Daily News* winning momentum in the community.

Successful ventures are always a lot of fun. The hours were long. Especially on Fridays when our small staff of about seven journalists put out the afternoon daily in the morning. We then turned around in the afternoon and evening to put out a Saturday morning paper. We put in 12-hour days. It made business sense, because people shop for cars, homes and big items over the weekend. Saturday morning is a good advertising slot. It was tough on our staff, but they hung in there because we were doing good work. The paper won lots of journalism awards. Ours is a self-congratulatory industry. We used the plaques to line the walls of the men's room.

No Do-Overs for Journalists

During my career as the editor of the *West Bend Daily News* in southeastern Wisconsin, I failed to head off a pedophile. Father Edmund Haen, the pastor of St. Francis Cabrini, West Bend's largest parish, a big man in town, had disappeared abruptly from the local scene. Rumors raced around the community.

I considered myself a serious, professional journalist, so I personally checked out the sensitive situation. Several members of the parish council, one a friend, refused to comment. No charges of any kind showed up. Haen was just gone — without explanation. I let myself get stonewalled by the church council and the diocese. Everyone clammed up.

My hunch and the rumors proved to be true. After his death, and following the big scandal that broke across the church, he was identified posthumously as a serial predator. The morally deficient heads of the Milwaukee archdiocese and parish had transferred him silently from West Bend to another parish in nearby Mequon, where his predation continued.

I didn't get the journalist's job done, and he went undisciplined and molested other boys. My friend on the parish council must have felt worse about our mutual lapse.

Epilogue: The legitimate claims against the Milwaukee Archdiocese, and its cover-up, drove it into a deserved bankruptcy in 2011. The unchecked pedophilia across the global church became an indelible stain. As so often happens in crises and scandals, the failure to cure the systemic rot and the cover-up proved as ugly as the initial crimes.

Thirty years later, a team of investigative journalists did a better job. They exposed the endemic cover-up in Boston and, later, other cities. Their work, for which they earned a Pulitzer Prize, became the subject of the Oscar-winning film, *Spotlight*.

I often wished I had the disappearance of Haen to do over again.

A BIG VENTURE THAT FAILED

Under the heading of "Be Careful What You Volunteer For," I got conscripted in 1975 to turn around an ambitious but failing attempt by Post Corporation to encircle *The Milwaukee Journal* and *Sentinel* with a group of suburban weeklies.

Post had a foothold in the Milwaukee metro market with the *West Bend Daily News* and a successful weekly in the *West Allis Post*, the largest of the suburban municipalities. Its manager got the big idea to create 12 free weekly newspapers, from the *North Shore Post* to the *Brookfield/Elm Grove Post* on the west side to the *Greenfield Post* on the south aside. (On the east side is Lake Michigan, so it was a horseshoe of weeklies.)

The suburbs were booming, while the central city was going the other way. A similar free weekly chain around St. Louis had taken away much of the advertising from the metro dailies, so there was a precedent for such a publishing adventure.

The powers-that-were at the Post headquarters in Appleton had grown unhappy with the losses at the Milwaukee start-up and asked me to step in as GM and editor. For better or worse, never one to turn down a challenge, I said, "Yes." It was the first step toward my eventual departure from Post Corporation, which I wanted to run one day.

Doing battle with Journal Communications, a half-billion dollar company, and its flagship paper, *The Milwaukee Journal*, had a Don Quixote feel to it. (Post Corp. had revenues of about $100 million.) The *Journal* had a distinguished newspapering history and was often ranked as one of the best dailies in the country. It was one of the first employee-owned corporations. People who worked there, including lowly paid news people, could buy stock with company-backed bank debt and retire in good financial shape when they sold their stock back to the company.

Our opposing business concept was solid. We would deliver one of 13 weeklies free to every home in the suburban area, thus offering advertisers 100 percent, coverage compared to about 50 percent penetration by the *Journal*. Each of our free papers carried loads of local news.

Further, we could give advertisers any combination of the 13 weeklies in Milwaukee and Waukesha counties, plus Washington and Ozaukee counties, the other two counties in the four-county metro area. They could, for example, buy just the North Side papers at a lower rate if they had a store only on the North Side.

We were sailing along toward a happy ending by 1977. Having landed one of the grocery chains and the biggest realtors with full-page weekly contracts, we broke into the black.

It had been an enormous effort. I was working long hours, six or seven days a week. My workaholic nature had returned to a nasty level, at the expense of my family.

Our circulation system had 2,000 young carriers, who were delivering to 220,000 homes — as much circulation as the *Journal* and more than the *Sentinel*, the morning paper. The carrier kids were great, but not always completely reliable. So a lot of management and systems were involved to make sure deliveries happened on time.

To keep our breakeven point low, the newsroom had just three seasoned editors: Audrey Dobish, Al Curtis and me. We had about 50 recent college grads as writers and editors, with part-time correspondents covering the various suburbs. They were energetic, but total rookies. It was pandemonium on deadline day.

Our composition and printing was done at the *Appleton Post-Crescent* 90 miles away. Again, Post wanted to do it on the cheap and hired rookies for off-hours page layout. That shortcut proved costly. There were some common pages for the 13 papers, but 400 were unique pages. That's a lot of composition and it left a lot of room for errors.

The kids up north left out the price of hamburger in a grocery ad one week. The placeholder awaiting the last-minute final price insertion into the ad was "$00." The real price never made the ad. Chaos followed, as all hands gathered over the weekend to rip that page out of the already printed paper. That would be 220,000 rip-outs — by hand.

I had tried but failed to get the composition moved to our shop in Milwaukee. It didn't happen and we lost the grocery advertiser. It was extremely frustrating.

Still, we were making hard-won progress in the face of growing competition. The *Journal* started some zoned ad buys. That we could have overcome.

8. Have Newsman's Trench Coat, Will Travel

What we couldn't overcome was the recession of 1979. The geniuses on Wall Street and in the nation's capital once again failed to see the signs coming. The country went into a substantial recession and soaring inflation. Paul Volcker's prescription from the Federal Reserve was to jack interest rates to get the inflation under control. It worked. He became a financial hero and sage.

His strategy was a disaster for Post Newspapers. Interest rates went to 22 percent at their high point. We had three main bases of advertising for our suburban papers: help wanted, car sales and real estate, all heavily dependent on interest rates. All three were in a tailspin and our advertising disappeared almost overnight.

What we had failed to foresee is that, because we were an alternative ad buy, our business was more fragile. The big advertisers pulled back on their ads in *The Journal*, maybe 10 to 25 percent, but they pulled our ads completely — to 0 percent.

The losses resumed. CEO Vic Minahan, my uncle, and CFO David Nelson, pulled the pin — after five years of ass-busting work. It was an understandable decision. We might have bounced back once the recession ended, but who knew?

Prior to that decision, Minahan and Nelson had decided that I needed to concentrate on the weeklies and yanked the *West Bend Daily News* from my management. I was furious. I needed Washington County for my metro four-county advertising buy. The twerp they sent down from Appleton to run the news immediately started playing games with the four-county buy.

He also started playing games with the females at the *Daily News* and had three sexual harassment charges in his first year there.

Pati and I spent a weekend with my parents, going primarily to my sensible mother for advice. I told her I was going to punch out Nelson next time I saw him. She advised me to quit, which I did abruptly the next day.

Vic and Nelson flew down to West Bend to try to talk me into staying. I had already decided, way down deep, that I didn't like the culture or ethics of the company dominated by Nelson's leadership. At the airport, I told them I was done for good.

After I quit in 1980, I soon realized I had no job, a wife and two kids, and little money in the bank. I applied for a lot of jobs but was turned down for many of them as "over-qualified."

Luckily, I had one place to invest my newspapering energies. Brothers Tom and Mark, fresh out of Dartmouth, decided to build a small newspaper operation. Tom and I had previously come close to buying the *Wausau Record-Herald*. We bid $5.5 million, with backing from Wausau Insurance and an inside track. In the 11th hour, it went to auction and sold to the *Green Bay Press-Gazette* for $7 million. Dang! (It flipped a few years later to Gannett for about $12 million. Dang — again!)

We lowered our sights and bought the *Menomonee (MI) Herald Leader*, perhaps the smallest daily in the country at 4,000 circulation. I had been a silent partner with Tom and Mark. But now out of a job, I had plenty of time to help, commuting from West Bend.

Tom and Mark had won lots of journalism awards and cleaned up on the advertising front with our free *Action* newspaper. We were having fun, bought the weeklies in Oconto and Gladstone, and created a successful shopper in Escanaba.

Our strategy or plan was to buy the competing *Marinette Eagle-Star* and combine the two dailies.

We were young, arrogant perhaps, and knew the newspaper business at the DNA level. Here's Tom's account of what happened: "In reflection, we won the battles and lost the war. I always regret that, as a young smart ass, I did not cultivate a respectful relationship with Fred Sappington, the elderly gentleman who had run the *Marinette Eagle-Star* for years and had the ear of the Mrs. Noyes, the old widow who owned it. He was a decent guy, very staid and traditional. He viewed us as interlopers, upstarts. I think he had planned to pick up the Menominee paper for peanuts and shut it down. If I could do it over again, I would join the country club, where he held sway, pay him proper obeisance, listen to him carefully and with respect. We might have had a different outcome. Ah, the folly of young ego."

Instead, Sappington engineered the sale to the *Janesville Gazette* owners, the Bliss family. They had deep pockets, cut ad rates to the bone and we were the losers. We sold to the Blisses, not the other way around.

There was a good ending.

Menominee had a long and terribly entrenched inferiority complex. In comparison with Marinette, it thought not much of itself. After seven or eight years, I think the recreation of a healthy, vibrant spirit of community was our main achievement. City government was alive again, with local election race hotly contested. Policy debates were public and thorough. Good things started happening. We got the decrepit downtown largely restored, including the rebuilding of the outer wall of the marina, which was the vital centerpiece of the downtown. It had been crumbling. Then came the restoration of blocks of historic buildings that lined the waterfront. Many creative new businesses sprung up in these buildings.

Brother Mark ended up as editor of the Janesville paper. I turned around Kondex Corp. and later became the business editor of the *Milwaukee Sentinel*. Tom became a spiritual teacher.

My trench coat and ambitions to be a foreign correspondent went dormant.

Editorial Postscript

BUSINESS LESSONS LEARNED:

- Be humble in business, never arrogant, which is inevitably fatal.

- Dig deep to find out what your customers really want and need. Listen hard.

- Build high-performance teams so you can win and enjoy every day at work.

- Create and display performance metrics that count.

- Spend your time and resources in rising marketplaces.

- You are not bulletproof, so take care of yourself and balance your work life with other dimensions.

- Scan the technology frontiers always to find game-changing innovations.

- Plagiarize successful business formulas and models from previous ventures. Dissect business obituaries for lessons.

CHAPTER 9

Encounters with Five Presidents:
NIXON WAS A LIAR, BUT "NOT A CROOK"

My classy first wife Pati Platten and I drove into the parking lot of the Ritz Carlton Hotel in the nation's capitol in our beat-up Dodge Aspen station wagon with a small U-Haul trailer in tow. It was the first Tuesday in November 1968. It was the grungiest car in the lot, by far. That should have been a tip-off.

We were arriving for a Congressional Fellowship that paid $14,000 for the year. The fancier cars belonged to the bigwigs in the Republican Party. The Ritz Carlton, we soon learned, was the headquarters for watching the 1968 election returns come in that night from across the country. We were smack in the middle of the country's quadrennial political crescendo.

It had been a traumatic year for the United States. Martin Luther King and Bobby Kennedy had been assassinated. Lyndon Johnson stepped back from a run for a full second term and stopped the bombing in Vietnam. Riots consumed the Democratic convention in Chicago as Hubert Humphrey was being nominated. George Wallace, the racial segregationist from Alabama, went on to win five southern states as an independent. (Wallace had become a national figure in the 1964 primaries when he won a shocking 34 percent of the Democratic votes in Wisconsin.) The nation was reeling in disarray.

My adventuresome wife never flinched from a challenge. I was selected as one of the eight journalists from across the country to spend a year on the inside of the workings of the nation's capitol. Journalists are outside the window pane, trying to figure out what's really going on with the other side in the halls of power. I was getting a chance to see the inside workings of our national government.

Pati and I were not accustomed to staying in swank hotels, but my newspaper employer had bartered a trade of advertising for our room. We were living above my pay grade.

After checking in, I made my way into its large convention hall and watched as Richard Nixon defeated Humphrey, the sitting vice president. The packed crowd of Republicans was in a very good mood.

After running a law and order campaign that appealed to what he called "the silent majority" of middle and working class Americans, Nixon won by less than one percent of the voters. He carried 32 states and 301 electoral votes, compared to 191 for Humphrey.

Wallace siphoned off wins in five states and 46 electoral votes, coming close to throwing the presidential election into the House of Representatives.

That morning, I reported in to the American Political Science Association to begin the fellowship, paid for by the Ford Foundation. We were there to learn the dynamics of Congress by working half the year in the House and the other half year in the Senate, with halves also divided evenly between Republicans and Democrats,

The eight Fellows were in demand because we were free help. The end game was that we were to return home as more knowledgeable journalists. Back then the press was viewed as "the Fourth Estate" behind the executive, legislative and judicial branches of government. It was considered a profession essential to a working democracy.

9. Encounters with Five Presidents

Most of us tried to be objective in our reporting to the people of the country. For that, we were worth educating.

Contrast that to the Trump campaign in 2016 against the press as "enemies of the people." I will contend always that reporters and editors are more "of the people" than a trust-fund brat who never had a callus on his hand, dodged the Armed Forces, and had inherited his fortune, then squandered it as a failed businessman.

I boiled my fellowship choices in the House down to Donald Rumsfeld of Illinois and George H. W. Bush of Texas. I really liked Bush, a fellow Yalie, but decided to go with Rumsfeld because he was a prime supporter of the fellowship program.

In retrospect, I should have chosen differently. Bush became the 41st president. But Rumsfeld, who went on to serve three times in a presidential cabinet, was a good choice, too. I always wondered whether I would have stayed in the halls of power if I had chosen Bush, with whom I would have been very compatible.

But Pati and I decided that we were deep-rooted Wisconsinites. We wanted to spend our lives where we had a rich history and fabric of friends and family. We drove back to the Wisconsin we loved after 13 months. I had served an extra month as GS15 civil servant as we waited the birth of our first son, Sean, born Sept. 23, 1969. As soon as he was three weeks old, we headed home.

There had been a chance that Sean would be born on the *Potomac*, the presidential yacht. The fellows were treated to a cocktail cruise on the Potomac River, during which Pati had labor pains and was allowed to lie down on the presidential bed. The pains subsided as we returned hastily to the dock.

The exposure to Congress, and later the executive branch, made me a more insightful reporter, editor and columnist. I had enjoyed a ringside seat to the inner sanctum of American politics.

My first day in Rummy's Congressional office, the day after the election, was an eye-opener. Every staff person but one loyalist was spending whole days on the phone trying to land a higher position in the new Nixon Administration. "Do you know someone who knows someone who could help me become deputy secretary of such and such department?"

Gaining power is the main game in D.C.

Most of them failed to move up and stayed put. I ignored their machinations and went to work on legislative issues and press releases.

Rumsfeld and other young GOP Turks were working to reform the seniority system that automatically made the longest serving committee member the chairman of the powerful commit-tees. Some were considered senile. In the end, the reformers got the system changed so committee members could choose from among three most senior on the committees. It was a small, but important, win.

My best piece of Congressional work for Rumsfeld was a push to end the draft. Conscription became controversial during the nasty Vietnam war and the GOP Turks decided to push for an all-volunteer armed forces.

The bill wasn't without pluses and minuses. It would move the services to a professional class, unleavened by the presence of civilians.

I had always propounded the virtue of ROTC programs, like the NROTC program I went through at Yale, because they added ordinary citizens to the officer corps as a balance to the young officers coming out of the academies. The ROTC graduates have broader palettes of education than allowed by the more narrow curricula of the academies.

A major minus for the volunteer system is that the services would lose their diverse make-up. Big chunks of society, like rich kids, could avoid the military. In my view, mandatory government service of some kind for young adults needs to be part of our national fabric.

I made the rounds of the Republican Congressional offices on The Hill and, working with their staffs, succeeded in convincing 70 members to sign on as co-sponsors. Rep. Bill Steiger of Oshkosh, the quarterback of the effort and Rumsfeld ally, became a friend.

That work in 1969 laid the groundwork for an historic, bipartisan ending of the draft five years later.

Meanwhile, President Nixon was having a tough time finding a Republican who wanted to take over the Office of Economic Opportunity (OEO), the agency created by President Johnson in 1964 to fight a "War on Poverty." It was being run by Sargent Shriver, who had married into the Kennedy family and had launched the Peace Corps. OEO was liberal bastion and wasn't the kind of place where a Republican could make a mark.

He turned to Rumsfeld, who held out and said he would only take the assignment if he could be in the Nixon cabinet. Nixon agreed.

It gave me the opportunity to go with him into the executive branch and see that side of the political world. I petitioned the American Political Science Association to shift branches and got the green light.

OEO was headquartered on K Street, the home of many powerful lobbying organizations. It had about 3,000 employees and budget of $3 billion. Rumsfeld, only 38, put together a team of six young bucks to run the diffuse organization: Frank Carlucci, Rummy's Princeton roommate—a seasoned civil servant who later became secretary of defense and chief of staff for President Reagan; Dick Cheney who later became vice president; Bill Bradley, the Princeton and New York Knicks basketball star who became a U.S. Senator from New Jersey and ran for presidency; Don Murdoch, an alderman from Madison who died young; Jim Leach, who went home and won a Congressional seat from Iowa and later headed the House Judiciary Committee; and me, the only one with management experience.

I got the press assignment in an agency of social engineers. News-wise, OEO was a sieve. The *Washington Post* would have multiple copies of internal memos the next day after they went out. Leaks from the department were rampant. I had never seen most of them.

Most Republicans wanted to dismantle OEO's array of poverty initiatives, including Head Start, Vista, Job Corps, and the Community Action Program. The *Post* was watching for any GOP cutbacks, so I had my hands full.

Rumsfeld surprised them all by going to the hill and going to bat for Head Start and for keeping OEO alive.

Many of the OEO programs were cloisters of good intentions, but management horror shows. Our program to train poor people to be commercial fishermen hit the rocks when two of its fishing vessels went missing. We found them abandoned on a beach in Bimini.

A TV production shop to train the poor as cameramen and production people in Los Angeles got shut down by the L.A. district attorney when the local newspaper discovered it was turning out porn films.

I was doing a lot of damage control.

My favorite assignment before I left for Wisconsin involved the Community Action Program in Puerto Rico. The Communist Party somehow had become the recipient of our federal funds for that program.

Carlucci, a former CIA operative, teamed me with a Spanish speaking CIA agent and we flew to San Juan. The governor's black limo was waiting for us at the airport and drove us straight to the governor's office. His whole cabinet was waiting there around a large table.

The governor was red in the face and pounding on the table. "How could you be so stupid?" he screamed.

I listened and came up with a solution. I arranged for the sponsorship of the program to be switched to the Catholic Church.

Long and short, I had a hoot in that year and became a smarter, wiser journalist.

Most of the OEO programs lived on in different agencies, but OEO was disassembled in the 1980s, long after Rummy had moved on.

The most important thing I learned was that most politicians make terrible managers. At least in the case of Rumsfeld, he was reluctant to trust anyone but his closest aides. Most private-sector managers bestow trust in their key people until proven untrust-worthy.

Rummy held his cards close to chest, so it was hard for agency executives, many highly trained and loyal to the incumbent's agenda, to figure out his direction.

That kind of criticism attached to Rumsfeld later when he twice ran the Pentagon.

That said, he was an energetic reformer and a very patriotic American. It was a privilege to work for him.

The funniest moment came after I wrote a speech for him to give to the state level poverty program directors. I had been trained as a journalist to use ground level words to communicate. Rummy liked abstractions and would often depart from my prepared talk and go into poverty jargon.

Tongue in cheek and a short-timer heading back to Wisconsin, I decided to write this last one with all abstractions and jargon. Afterward, he bounced into the small office that housed Leach, Bradley, Murdoch and me, and yelled: "Who wrote that speech?"

Oh, oh, I went too far. I slowly raised my hand.

Said Rummy, "I loved it."

Encounters with Five Presidents

The No-Nonsense Harry S. Truman

Journalism pays very poorly, but it does offer a close-up seat to history in the making.

After 25 years in news rooms, I was making $50,000 per year as business editor and columnist for the *Milwaukee Sentinel*, the highest paid guy on the staff actually writing. The other editors, who didn't write much, made a little more. Writing is hard work, so most news guys are more than happy to stop writing after they are elevated to mostly anonymous editor jobs.

Harry S. Truman, 33rd President.

9. Encounters with Five Presidents

My two decades in the journalism playpen put me close up to three presidents, a dozen governors, lots of CEOs and an unending stream of interesting people. My definition of a good day is when you get to meet, interact and converse with a fascinating person or two.

Even before my time in the newsroom, I met Harry S. Truman when he was a visiting Chubb Fellow at Timothy Dwight College at Yale. I was president of the residential college's student council, so I was selected to be his campus guide.

Truman was the same down-to-earth, no-nonsense man in person as he was in public, and he might have answered my question with some of his patented plain talk.

THE AFFABLE RONALD REAGAN

Ronald Reagan came through West Bend, Wisconsin, where I ran the local paper, when he was making his first run for president in 1968. The former actor and governor of California was also down to earth. He wore a rumpled trench coat and had four or five

Ronald Reagan, 40th President.

well-worn newspapers under his arm. He was obviously well versed on the news of the day. That impression — of a man who was up on the issues — stuck with me as his opponents over the years tried to paint him as a dim fellow. He had been head of his actors' guild and union members don't pick dimwit negotiators. Dimwits don't read five newspapers a day.

Reagan's visit gave me the inside track on Sam Donaldson, the confrontational, big-time TV newsman and the rest of the national press corps. Donaldson was on the outside looking in when Reagan and a couple dozen Rotarians met over lunch at the old Washington House, once West Bend's main hotel, but then a bedraggled apartment building with a big dining room. Because I was local, I was the only newsman allowed in the dining room. I could see Sam peering in through a glass door.

The hotel served chicken cordon bleu about noon to all the guests. The secret service men had locked up Reagan's portion of the chicken dish the night before. They padlocked the refrigerator to avoid tampering.

Reagan and his entourage were about a half hour late and the guests didn't want to eat ahead of him. Their chicken cordon bleu (layers of pastry, chicken and cheese) slowly congealed as they waited.

When Reagan arrived, my newsman's curiosity almost got me shot. I was two tables away and got up to see if Reagan's food was the same as ours. I took a couple steps toward his table to get a better look. Two guys in dark suits jumped up and reached toward their chest holsters. I sat back down quickly.

I always wondered what would have happened if I had taken another step or two.

Reagan lost to Richard Nixon in November 1968, but went on to win when he ran again in 1980.

9. Encounters with Five Presidents

I experienced him close up one more time in 1987, near the end of his presidency. I was invited to a Reagan press conference for regional economic writers at the Executive Office Building in Washington, DC. His press people must have figured the President would get more favorable treatment from us than from the Washington press corps.

It was looking like an uneventful exchange, except that the president stumbled badly with some of his answers. He looked affable, as always, but confused. About 15 minutes into the conference, Frank Carlucci, his chief of staff, with whom I had worked in 1969 during my D.C. fellowship, came to the lectern, took the President by the arm and led him off stage. Carlucci came back and finished the Q&A.

Clearly — to me anyway — President Reagan was mentally impaired. His limitations in his last year in office was never widely reported in the press. When I returned home, I wrote about his condition in my column in the *West Bend Daily News*, circulation 14,000. No one else was writing about his mental decline.

After his presidency, his Alzheimer's disease was made public. It grew worse when he was out of office and Reagan died of its complications in June 2004. Later studies of his language patterns by researchers showed that he indeed had started to show the effects of the disease while still President.

So, the U.S. had been headed by a mentally impaired leader for more than a year. His staff and wife Nancy kept his condition under wraps. Did she do the country a service or disservice? My guess is that Carlucci, who later served as Secretary of Defense, was making many of the presidential decisions. Fortunately, he was a very competent public servant.

Nixon "Not a Crook"

I was about 20 feet away from President Richard Nixon when he uttered the sad words: "I am not a crook; I am not a crook."

It was during a press conference in front of the Associated Press Managing Editors' convention in D.C. in November 1973. The Providence, Rhode Island, newspaper had published articles showing that Nixon had paid almost no income taxes for the prior two years. He had taken big deductions for the donation of his presidential papers to his future library. It was a questionable deduction.

I remember seeing Nixon's contorted body and the sweat on his forehead as he answered the questions about his taxes. I had been late arriving at the conference and the place was already full. So seats were added on the stage and I got one of them — 20 feet from the embattled President.

The President turned in my direction and almost seemed to be pleading for sympathy. His body language made him look guilty as hell.

At that time, he was also facing questions about the Watergate break-in, so this was one more blow to his presidency. He was badly wounded politically. His opponents in politics and the press were on his bloodied trail.

A year later, faced with impeachment charges, Nixon, a most complicated man, resigned as president.

Richard M. Nixon, 37th President.

9. Encounters with Five Presidents

I LIKED IKE

I never met Dwight Eisenhower, but was in the crowd lining Pennsylvania Avenue when Ike's horse-drawn casket rolled by in 1969. It was the classic military, presidential funeral. Most memorable was the riderless horse with the boots backwards in the stirrups that follows all presidential funerals.

Dwight D. Eisenhower, 34th President.

BUSH: PREPARED FOR THE PRESIDENCY

George H. W. Bush was a congressman when I met him in late 1968 at the beginning of my Congressional Fellowship. We were free help, so House members were eager to recruit us in return for sharing their experiences.

He entered the room to address the eight fellows, took off his jacket, loosened his tie and easily engaged the group. I really liked him, not because he was a Yalie, but because he came off as a regular guy — an accomplished man without airs.

My middle name is Bush, a family name on my dad's maternal side. My son Sean checked out the possible links with H.W. and it turns out that he and I are 11th cousins.

The separate Bush families hit New York from Britain within years of each other in the late 1790s. Our Bush family ended up in Battle Creek, Michigan, in the manufacturing business. None of our Bush family, except Sean as a young man, ever ran for office.

George H. W. Bush, 41st President.

H.W. was arguably the most prepared President in modern times. He had been:

- *Summa cum laude* at Yale
- A World War II hero shot down twice
- Representative and Senator
- An entrepreneurial Texas oil man
- Head of the CIA
- Ambassador to China
- Vice President under Reagan

He was a far better president than generally recognized.

9. Encounters with Five Presidents

SHIRLEY, THE FOX

I also had the pleasure of covering Shirley MacLaine when she was stumping for Bobby Kennedy in West Bend in 1968. She was a fox, as beguiling in person as on screen. Who wouldn't love her, even if she was a notorious flake who believed in reincarnation?

"VICE" HAS FEW VIRTUES

Having worked side by side with Dick Cheney and Donald Rumsfeld way back in 1968-69, I was anxious in 2018, 50 years later, to see how Hollywood would depict them in the just-released movie, *Vice*. Not surprisingly, given the groupthink politics of Hollywood, both came off in a very negative light.

The opening scenes show Cheney being arrested on a DUI and participating in a barroom brawl. They quickly establish that he was a Yale dropout. The tough carouser portrayal doesn't square with the Cheney I drank a few beers with when he was in his late 20s. He wasn't a big man; he wasn't very muscular and he didn't drink a lot. The young Cheney I knew was personally affable, not at all pugnacious.

He was smart, determined, and already a political operative. That started in Wisconsin. After graduating with a baccalaureate from the University of Wyoming in his home state, he started a Ph.D. program at UW–Madison, but didn't finish. He switched to political work for Wisconsin Republican Gov. Warren Knowles.

He was always a conservative. He didn't switch opportunistically when he hit D.C., as the film contends.

We were both Congressional Fellows and ended up side by side in Rumsfeld's office. Therein lies another distortion in the film. Rumsfeld, who was close to the American Political Science Association, is shown addressing the new fellows and repeatedly using off-color language.

For 13 months, I served as his press aide in Congress and later in the Nixon Cabinet when he was picked to run the poverty program. I can't remember him using coarse language. He may have, but I never heard it.

The film's main message was that Rumsfeld and Cheney, political allies for more than three decades, were all about seeking and holding power, not about doing the right stuff. They certainly were very ambitious.

Let's not be naïve, though. Seeking power is a way of life in Washington, D.C. At least half the denizens of the halls of the Capitol are on the make for higher positions. It's not all bad. If a politician has some passions for certain causes, he or she gets a lot more done when in the driver's seat than when not.

Power is like money. It can be put to good use or otherwise.

When President Nixon plucked Rumsfeld out of the House to head the Office of Economic Opportunity, Rummy insisted on being in the Cabinet. He took a couple of months to assess the myriad of programs created by the social engineers in the van- guard of the war on poverty. Then he went to the Hill and used his chits with congressional friends on both sides of the aisle to save Head Start.

He also sanctioned experiments with a negative income tax and a contraception program in Appalachia. The film depicts Rummy as smarmy and conniving. I saw a real guy, plenty smart enough, who wanted to reform every organization he led.

By the time I left, Cheney was his head staffer as they worked to stave off GOP efforts to disband the entire poverty agency.

Despite the opportunity to stay in the halls of power, I returned to Wisconsin as a newsman. So I wasn't there as Cheney and Rumsfeld rose even higher to roles as defense secretaries, chiefs of staff, and Cheney to "Vice."

They were not hyper-partisan or neo-cons as young men, but they hardened their views of the world after serving as defense secretaries. The daily security briefings must have scared the hell out of them. They were determined to quell the terrorist bases of support in the world. After 9/11 they were obsessed with anti-terrorism.

You can argue they overreacted, but you aren't sitting in their hot seats.

It is my best explanation for why they made the strategic blunder of going to war in Iraq in 2003. By almost all accounts, it was a colossal mistake that further destabilized the Middle East and cost many lives.

They didn't learn from President H.W. Bush, who went into Kuwait with good intelligence, defined objectives, a solid international alliance, support from Congress, and a defined exit plan. H.W. got in, kicked butt and got out.

Their miscalculation recalls why and how we got into the Vietnam war. The best and brightest, "the whiz kids," like Defense Secretary Robert McNamara, over-reacted to the spread of communism. When JFK stood up to the Russians over Berlin, it had to be done to protect the independence of Europe. With the benefit of hindsight, getting involved in what turned out to be a civil war in Vietnam did not. It was an over-reaction.

In his first campaign, George W. Bush said he never wanted to be a nation builder. He was right. Yet, his close advisers Cheney and Rumsfeld got him into that business. We were still in Afghanistan in 2021 when President Biden finally exited.

That said, the producers of *Vice* executed a hit job on two long-serving patriotic Americans, who together made a lot of good calls, along with one big, bad one in Iraq.

Fortunately, there were only three other people in the small Hartford, Wisconsin theater the night I watched the defamation called *Vice*.

9. Encounters with Five Presidents

EDITORIAL POSTSCRIPT

The decisions to go to war are perilous, and, too often, as in Vietnam and Iraq 2003, turn out to be monstrous mistakes.

Over my life, I have developed six litmus tests that need to be passed to justify releasing the dogs of war:

1. There needs to be a clear and present danger to American lives and overriding national interests.

2. Our leaders must have developed the support of the American people.

3. We must have gained the support of our international allies.

4. We must be able to go in with overwhelming force; winning is the only option

5. We must have an exit plan.

6. Congress must vote to approve sending out troops into war.

Dick "D.C." Bambenek made an enormous imprint on me.
I loved him and I respected his warmth and entrepreneurial guts.

CHAPTER 10

Winona, Peerless Chain,
Bub's Beer, and a Failed Takeover:
GRANDPA'S GOOD CHEER AND BUSINESS SMARTS

om's dad, Dominic C. Bambenek, proudly toured Tom and me through his company, Peerless Chain Company in Winona, Minnesota. He stopped at every metal-bending machine to say hello to "his boys." The workers would shake D.C.'s hand with big smiles. They loved the man. My decision to study Industrial Administration, a combination of business and engineering, at Yale came from knowing that grand man.

D.C. never finished grade school and was working as a haberdasher when a guy came through town with a patent for making a cross-linked tire chain. His older brother Joe bought the patent. Joe, D.C. and Al, the youngest and trained in accounting, became entrepreneurs. They started the company in 1917. Al and Joe went off to World War I, while D.C. kept the fledging company going. Their dad, John Bambenek, helped in the shop. When the two brothers returned from Europe, Joe became general manager, Al did finance and D.C., also known as Dick, led the sale of stock in the company, going door to door. He came up with the idea of selling $100 shares on credit, with $10 down and $10 installments. D.C. became president, but served mainly as the CEO. The brothers started with two metal bending and welding machines on the second floor of a butcher shop on the Polish east end of Winona.

Molly Torinus at the old Peerless plant.

By the time D.C. led Tom and me through the corporate headquarters and the main plant after World War II, it had grown to 350 employees, including brother Chester, who ran the parts department; Lambert, a machine operator; sister Madge, an inspector; and brother-in-law Eddie Joswick, also a machine operator. The plant was in an old three-story, red brick building on the banks of the Mississippi River.

Dick used to call major snowfalls across the nation "white gold." Peerless would fill its warehouse with inventories of tire chains — long before snow tires were invented and lean inventory theories. When storms hit the northern states, train cars full of product would stream out of Winona and the profits poured in.

The three Bambenek brothers were very close and extremely proud of Peerless. Their summer cottages were next door to each other in nearby Minneiska on the banks of the Mississippi River.

I worked there the summer after Grandma Anna died in 1953. Anna and D.C. had been married 48 years and Dick, normally a jolly man, went into depression. He started drinking heavily. Anna had ruled the domestic roost and kept D.C., who liked a good time, in line. I was 17, and Mom thought if I lived with him that summer, he would behave better. That didn't work out so well. He would take me to the Winona "A.C." (a Polish-American athletic club where I didn't see much evidence of athleticism), order himself a shot with a beer and me a tap beer.

Grandpa Dick had invested in the local Bub's Brewery as it was starting to fail. Every town of any size had its own brewery in those days. Bub's, like other local breweries across the country, was succumbing to the big advertising budgets of major breweries like Budweiser, Miller, Pabst and Schlitz. D.C. stepped in as Bub's president and most loyal customer. Its brew master was Peter Bub (pronounced *boob*). The motto on the Bub's label was: "It makes it fun to be thirsty." Later vernacular would make that motto pretty amusing.

The brewery resided just under the city's signature geological form, a 500-foot limestone outcropping called The Sugar Loaf, which looks like a top hat on the Mississippi bluffs. Six caves carved into the bluffs served as cool warehouses for beer kegs and cases, with temperatures at a steady 45 degrees.

After D.C. died in 1969, the brewery died, too, 113 years after its start. The brand survived and was resurrected 30 years later at Bub's Pub, a micro-brewery in downtown Winona.

My job at Peerless that summer was material handler and light machine operator. I used to get really dirty and greasy from the oil-slicked steel coils, our basic raw material. I would get cleaned up after work and D.C. would let me borrow his tomato-red Chrysler Imperial for an occasional date. It was *nouveau riche*, but did he or I care? He loved that car, so did I. It had big chrome ornaments on the rear fenders.

Out of boredom, I remember quadrupling the rate on the wire-forming machine I was running. It was turning out end pieces for retail chain reels, still found in hardware stores 50 years later. I wasn't on piece rate, where you get paid by the

Peerless Chain Company, 1941.

Peerless tire chain.

volume of parts you produce, but I was inherently interested in productivity. The foreman in the unionized plant came up to me and said in a low voice, "Slow down, kid; you're going to work yourself out of a job."

I realized back then that unions were not looking to make companies more profitable or competitive. They were making a big mistake. There had to be better employee -employer models. Fifty years later, unions had all but disappeared from the private sector in the U.S. — only 9 percent of the U.S. work force. Their adversarial philosophy had made unions an anachronism at Peerless. But Dick's positive relationship with his workers had carried forward. Its union was not a problem.

In 1994, I returned to Winona and Peerless as a member of the board of directors. The company was in big trouble because cheap imports were starting to come into the country. Peerless was going to have to learn to take on global competition.

10. Winona, Peerless Chain, Bub's Beer...

The CEO at the time was Mom's first cousin-in-law, James Jerecyk, who married Joe Bambenek's daughter Irene. He had been a haberdasher before joining Peerless. After the three founding brothers had passed, Jerecyk put five cronies on the board, along with himself and Uncle Ray. He put me on the board when Ray passed. He told me later, "Putting you on the board was the biggest mistake I ever made." From his perspective, I agreed. From mother's, it was the best thing that could have happened. Jerecyk knew little about manufacturing and the company was spiraling downward. My mother's significant inheritance from D.C. and Ann was melting away.

It was a tough period on the board. The votes were invariably 6-1, with me in the minority. I opposed most of the measures that Jerecyk proposed. He just didn't get manufacturing. His cronies went along.

As matters worsened, I decided to force the sale or takeover of the company. It was a public company, even though the three prongs of the founding Bambenek family still owned a majority.

I had always gotten along well with Jim Frankard, VP of engineering, Al's son-in-law, a board member, and a former Air Force pilot. He had installed the company's automated electro-plating line and was proud of it. It was a pretty clean system as far as electroplating went. He had married Jean Bambenek, Al's only child and a close cousin of Mom's.

With Jim's votes, we could have formed a majority coalition to take out Jerecyk. But Jim was a mild-mannered guy who didn't like confrontation, even though he agreed with me on most business matters. I couldn't tip him to go against the grain, so the votes remained 6-1.

My next move was to hire Roger Minahan, a shark lawyer and distant relative who had been counsel for Post Corp. With his help, I mounted a takeover offer of $21 per share, a little above where Peerless had been trading on the unlisted stock market. One of Jerecyk's many mistakes had been to take the small company public.

Jerecyk preferred any option other than my taking over. So, without an investment banker, another mistake, he brought in a small private equity company called Kidd, Kamm and Associates. He sold the company to them for $24 per share.

I had been prepared to pay more than that, but — my mistake — didn't have the capital lined up to get into a bidding war.

Further, Mom had only one-sixth of the Bambenek block. Her brother Ray's estate had another one-sixth, but it was controlled by a trustee at a local bank where Jerecyk was a director.

My main objective had always been to protect Mom's value in Peerless. So she and I decided to go along with the deal. We extracted about $2 million in the sale, and that sum gave our family a lot of financial security. Thanks, D.C. and Anna.

The end result was even better. Ray, who was childless and close to Louise and John, left 80 percent of his estate to my five siblings and me. Mother used part of her proceeds, $300,000, to help me buy Serigraph in 1987.

As for Peerless, Kidd, Kamm flipped it five years later. It has been sold three more times since. The last sale was in 2014 to a Japanese company, Kito Corp., for about $150 million. It is still prospering, a century after the three Bambenek brothers founded their company in east Winona.

I took my then-seven-year-old granddaughter Molly there in 2015. She was interested in factories and how things are made.

Molly, her parents, Dan and Ingrid, and I also took a trip to the Keshubia region of Poland in 2016 to find the Bambenek roots. It was exciting to see how far Poland had come since escaping the Soviet yoke in 1989.

We learned why Martin Bambenek and his wife Magdalena, D.C.'s grandparents, loaded their nine kids on a schooner in 1868 and headed for the United States. They fled the barren soils southwest of Gdansk on the Baltic Sea for the rich lands, forests, lakes and rivers of Wisconsin and Minnesota. The family quickly acclimated and eventually earned prosperity through Peerless.

Editorial Postscript

With not much to lose, the three Bambenek brothers had the guts to launch a company with almost no start-up capital. They believed in themselves, and so did the people of Winona, Minnesota. The brothers treated their workers well. It all worked and a successful venture became an American success story. Entrepreneurs were the country's heroes then, and they still are today. They re-invent the economy as the older firms fade into history.

My dad always wore his tie at half-mast in the newsroom. So did I. He wrote several thousand columns over a 50-year career. So did I. Instead of anonymous editorials, we personalized our opinions — and took the heat personally.

Business editor, 1983, *Milwaukee Sentinel*, 1987

The logo for my columns.

CHAPTER 11

A Sayonara Gig in the Newsroom:
How to Get Fired

My cousin Mike Walter and I made a run in 1983 at convincing our parents, my dad and Aunt Mary Walter, to use their stock in Post Corp. to retain family ownership in the *Appleton Post-Crescent* and the *West Bend News*. We hired a big-time Chicago law firm to help, but Dad and Mary had to think about themselves and their other 11 children. So, they went along with the sale of Post Corp. to George Gillett, who, despite promises to the contrary, promptly resold the newspapers to the Thompson chain, which publishes some of the weakest papers in North America. He kept the TV properties.

Post Corp. had been selling on the public market for small companies at $21 to $23 per share for more than a decade. Gillett paid $65, still below its real value.

With hindsight, three decades later, it proved to be a smart time to sell. Our forebears sold at the high point of newspaper values, which went into a tailspin as the Internet kicked into high gear in the 1990s. Newspapers were selling out to the chains then at 40 times earnings or four times revenues, huge multiples in recognition of their high margins and near monopoly status. By 2015, papers were folding, down-sizing and selling for values at 25 percent of their peak. The Minahan and Torinus families, no thanks to me, dodged the Internet bullet by selling at the top.

Were they clairvoyant? Probably not. Our parents were at the end of their careers and it was time to cash out.

115

On my end, after selling Kondex and Menominee Publishing by 1983, I was out of work. I spent eight months looking for a job, but was often "over-qualified, — too old at 46 and too expensive.

It was pretty demoralizing, and I had a wife and two kids to support. My meager reserves were dwindling.

My wife Pati noticed a small article in the *Milwaukee Sentinel* that its business editor had resigned. I was looking to get back into action, so I said, "What the hell? I can do that job; I've been in business, unlike most business journalists, and I've been an editor."

I put my butt in a chair and banged out three columns on the Wisconsin economy. In those days, we had typewriters and cheap copy paper. That was the format. I made them look like they were just off the typewriter, fresh with black pencil edits. In actuality, I'd had two fine editors, my dad and brother Tom, edit them hard. They looked like a first cut, but were letter perfect.

The day after *Sentinel* editor Bob Wills received them, he called me for an interview and I was hired on the spot. It was the start of a stimulating four-year trip through Wisconsin business — the equivalent of an MBA.

Indeed, I had started an Executive MBA program at UW–Milwaukee in August, but had to drop out when I started the *Sentinel* job in October. With kids still at home, and what turned out to be a 60-hour-per-week position, there was no way I could keep up, or even catch up, with the younger MBA students. I bailed on grad school to take a job that paid $36,000 a year. There I was, with 20 years of editing experience and an advanced degree, making about $12 an hour.

But I was back in the news game.

Unlike the other *Sentinel* editors, and unlike the business editor at *The Milwaukee Journal*, I wasn't above writing. I covered some stories and wrote two to three columns per week. I became a minor celeb in the Milwaukee business world.

We had only six journalists on the *Sentinel* business staff, compared to 16 at the afternoon *Journal*, the mothership. But, we had the morning news slot, a big advantage. Most business news breaks after 10 a.m. in a work day — too late for the deadline for the p.m. paper.

Wills liked breaking news, hard news stories, scoops, so that's what we gave our readers. The *Sentinel*'s circulation was about 160,000 when I got there and was approaching 200,000 by the time I left four years later. Meanwhile, The *Journal* was dropping fast, desperately trying to stay above the 300,000 mark. The collapse of print journalism had just started. From covering about a half-million homes in the Milwaukee market between the *Journal* and the *Sentinel* — about two of every three — the combined circulation would drop to one of three 30 years later. By 2017, the merged *Journal Sentinel* daily circulation had collapsed to 84,000, one-sixth of the high point.

Inside that falling dynamic in the 1980s, the *Sentinel* was on the rise and the popularity of our business pages was part of the up-tick.

"Why not break business news out as a separate section?" I asked Wills. "The section will draw business-to-business advertisers." He agreed, and it worked.

My second week on the job, I traveled north to Oshkosh to a business convention at the Pioneer Resort. Gov. Tony Earl was the keynote speaker and he floated a trial balloon proposing a flat personal income tax for the state. No other journalist was there, so I had a scoop. I called the story into the city desk, dictating from the top of my head.

"Are you sure he said that?" asked an unbelieving city editor. (I had scooped the paper's political writers.)

"I'm sure."

They took the story to Wills and he told them to go with it. It was the top line, not of the business page, but page one — in 60-point type. It was a nice start.

Our staff dug out many more stories that the *Journal* couldn't touch. We neutralized their staff advantage by convincing other writers in the newsroom that they could get big play for their pieces on my pages. So we picked up stories from the court reporters; the Madison bureau, where the interaction between the business world and government was constant; and the suburban and upstate reporters. We also established a network of correspondents from journalists I knew across the state. We had a field day.

Our reporting helped send the Newman brothers of Green Bay to jail for bilking old-timers of their savings. They used Christian prayer meetings to gain access to elders and their investment accounts. (Johnny Brogan, a boyhood friend and broker in the Fox Valley, gave me the tips on that saga.) Moral of that story: When business people mix in religion, put your hand on your wallet.

In my columns, I pushed hard for economic development in Wisconsin, for a reinvention of the economy and for job creation. I could see that the state's dependence on agri-business and manufacturing was not sustainable. Those two sectors were becoming extraordinarily efficient and productive. Their production could keep growing, even in the face of global competition, but their employment numbers would continue to drop.

Less than two percent of the population was able to feed the entire country, to a point of an obesity epidemic, and much of the rest of the world as well. Ditto for the trend in manufacturing, which employed 30 percent of the population in 1950. It was nine percent by 2015 in the country and 18 percent in Wisconsin. It would not be but a few decades when five percent of the population would be able to make all the goods Americans could consume.

I gave dozens of speeches on economic development, partly to promote the *Sentinel*, but also to get the message out. (In the process, I worked to become a good speaker, a skill that was later to help me toward another career.)

The paper sent me to Japan for six weeks and China for two in the mid-1980s to get a first-hand look at the competitive pressures that those two countries were bringing to bear on the United States and Wisconsin, especially on manufacturing. My wife Pati was great support during my absence for those adventures.

Wills submitted my two series for Pulitzers, but I never got the gold ring.

As part of my reporting, I visited a three-cow dairy farm in Japan, where every dropping was quickly scooped up for fertilizer. The barn was immaculate. The farm was unsustainable, but Japanese politicians protected its small farmers from dairy imports from the U.S. Back in Wisconsin, the dairy industry was moving to corporate farms of hundreds, even thousands, of cows.

Mike Mansfield, U.S. ambassador to Japan, slipped me a story that the U.S. trade deficit would hit a staggering $36 billion in 1984. I filed the "scoop" from the Tokyo bureau of Associated Press, but it drew a big yawn, only short stories, back home. By 2000, the trade deficit grew to more than that each month. The biggest factor in the soaring deficit was the imbalance with China, which was using cheap labor and an under-valued currency, the yuan, to produce double-digit growth — at the expense of American jobs.

Harvey Wilmeth, chief economist for Northwestern Mutual Life, the nation's largest life insurer, took me to lunch and introduced his concept of "balanced trade" between nations. That would mean China exports to the U.S. would have to be matched to U.S. exports to China. I wrote in support and even got Russ Darrow, a friend, to introduce the concept in his race for the Wisconsin Republican nomination for the U.S. Senate.

At a Yale reunion, I put that idea to classmate Winston Lord, former U.S. ambassador to China and every bit the East Coast patrician that his name implied. He blew me off. "I don't believe in bilateral trade agreements," he sniffed. "I only believe in multi-lateral agreements."

Flash forward 25 years and the China trade deficit was still growing, to more than $350 billion per year. Mansfield would have been appalled.

Lord, it turned out, was dead wrong. Warren Buffet, the world's greatest investor, ratified bilateral balanced trade by proposing in *Fortune Magazine* just such a chit system. The trade debate later raged into the 2016 presidential campaign, unsolved for lack of politicians seeing and understanding the Wilmeth/Buffet pragmatic solution.

Donald Trump rode the issue in a populist campaign, all the way to the presidency. On taking office, he pursued greater trade equality using the sledge hammer of higher tariffs across the board. The Chinese pushback unsettled the global economy.

Trump failed to realize that American consumers would be the ones paying the import tax on Chinese goods. Wisconsin farmers suffered greatly from the counter-tariffs on agricultural products like soybeans. Unsolved trade and military issues continued to stress the relationships with China. Those testy dynamics were certain to persist for many years to come.

The U.S. trade deficit with China and the rest of the world actually increased during Trump's first and only term.

11. A Sayonara Gig in the Newsroom

BACK TO THE NEWSROOM

Making stars of our writers was one of the best methods I came up with to build followership for our business pages. Avi Lank became a columnist on personal finance, with his face on every weekly column. It would define the rest of his career. Al Curtis wrote a column on real estate. Lee Bergquist became our expert on the interests of business and government in the environmental arena.

One of my favorite pieces of reporting was on the surprise raid by CEO Roger Fitzsimmons of First Wisconsin Bank on CEO George Slater at Marine Bank. I had been on the board of West Bend Marine Bank, so I knew Slater, and he gave me a blow-by-blow, almost minute-by-minute account of the attempted takeover, starting with him in his pajamas on a Saturday morning on the phone with Fitzsimmons. The Fitzsimmons takeover failed when Slater found another suitor in Chase Bank. It was great copy — an insider report.

Then, one of my young reporters busted the story of CEO Darwin Smith's 1986 decision to move the headquarters of Kimberly-Clark to Plano, Texas, from its historic location in Neenah, Wisconsin. Smith severely criticized the anti-business climate in Wisconsin as he orchestrated his move. It touched off a political firestorm in a state that was seeing a serious erosion of its traditional manufacturing base.

Smith gave me an exclusive interview as grist for my columns. I think he trusted my even-handedness and liked that I hailed from the Fox River Valley, then the paper-making capital of the world.

In the end, Smith did move the K-C headquarters to Texas, despite entreaties from Gov. Tony Earl, but it involved only 50 top executive jobs. Even R&D stayed in Neenah.

121

From his detached perch in Plano, Smith eventually exited paper making. He sold K-C's paper mills and transformed the company into a consumer products winner with brands like Kleenex, Depends and Pampers.

Smith gave gravitas to the debate on economic development by funding a major survey of Wisconsin business. Its negative findings on the state's business climate, which the *Sentinel* covered intensively, kicked off a 30-year drive to improve job creation and the business climate in the state. Earl lost his next race to Tommy Thompson, a pro-business GOP legislator, who would win an unprecedented four terms. The jobs issue was the deciding factor.

Three decades later, job creation was still the number one issue in the governor's race in 2014. The *Sentinel*'s business pages advanced that important dialog.

During my four years as business editor, I often said of Wisconsin's lagging economy, with its long list of failing companies and a 40-year slide in terms of share of U.S. GDP: "I feel more like an obituary writer than a business journalist."

My staffs covered the demise of Allis Chalmers, Schlitz, Blatz, Pabst, Crucible Steel, the West Bend Company, Amity Leather Products, McQuay-Perfex, and many more.

We were reporting on a macro-economic shift: the hollowing out of "the Rust Belt," a nasty description of a manufacturing sector, even though it still held enormous strengths.

Nonetheless, it was very clear that Wisconsin had to reinvent its economy.

By 1987, I was getting antsy. I was tired of working for other people. That meant leaving my chosen profession. But there was to be one more kick at newspapering.

11. A Sayonara Gig in the Newsroom

BREACH OF JOURNALISM ETHICS

About ten years after I left the *Sentinel* in 1987 to buy Serigraph, the editors of the merged *Journal Sentinel* called to see if I would write a column on business, finance, and economics for the Sunday paper. I did that for about a dozen years — until I got fired by editor Martin Kaiser.

That termination was a major case study in journalism ethics — or the lack thereof.

Journal Communications Inc. (JCI) had gone public in 2003 to solve a problem with the stock loans its employees had taken on. The employees had held control of the corporation through one of the country's first employee-owned plans. The price on the public offering was $15 per share and it rose as high as $20. (I sold my few shares when I left the still-private company in 1987, with a nice but small profit.)

Many employees and retirees, despite the opportunity to diversify, rolled their old ownership units into the new publicly traded shares. That meant they still had big bank loans from when they originally bought units.

The company had always paid high dividends — more than enough to cover the debt service on their loans. That nifty arrangement unraveled in 2008 when newspapers took big hits to their advertising revenues amidst the Great Recession. In many ways, that economic collapse was more severe than the Great Depression from 1929 to 1939.

Steve Smith, *Journal* CEO, had been led by the nose by the geniuses at Robert W. Baird & Company, the state's biggest investment banker, and Foley & Lardner, the state's biggest law firm, into a series of acquisitions, mostly TV and radio stations. He took on tons of debt. Smith leveraged the $600 million revenue company with $350 million in loans, a dangerous level by any standard.

The lethal combination of falling revenues and heavy debt service caused a precipitous fall in JCI's stock price to 39 cents a share.

It was a disaster for employee and retiree shareholders. Their loans went under water, the point where their debt exceeded the value of their shares. Banks called the loans, and people I had worked with lost their life savings. It was especially tough on retirees; some had to go back to work. Some still owed the banks a balance after their shares were forced to be sold.

In the midst of that mess, several retirees asked me and two others, the former corporate counsel, Paul Kritzer, and the former banking reporter, Doug Armstrong, to run as dissident directors for JCI's nine-person public-company board. I called Smith to be straight-forward about my decision. He was extremely hostile.

His buddies at the Foley & Lardner law firm figured out a way to keep us off the proxy, which meant the three of us would have to run a proxy fight for an estimated $1.5 million. We didn't have the dough, so that was the end of that.

If we had gotten on the proxy, we were a cinch to be elected. Each employee share carried 10 votes, more than enough for a majority. Comically, Smith put out a press release saying that the three of us were "unqualified," despite our combined 75 years in the media business. His board had one media professional.

Subsequently, a reporter for *Milwaukee Magazine*, Mary Vandekamp-Knoll, called me to ask for an analysis on the JCI meltdown. I refused, because I was still writing the Sunday *Journal Sentinel* column.

She kept calling and I finally agreed to an interview on the promise that it was completely off the record. She agreed and I gave her a dissection of the strategic errors Smith had made that led to the demise of the once-proud enterprise.

11. A Sayonara Gig in the Newsroom

Six months went by with no article. Then I got a call from Editor Kaiser. "John, I don't like what you said in an article."

"What article?" I'm thinking, caught flat-footed.

"We're going to have to let you go," said Kaiser, not elaborating.

"Let me dig into it and I'll call you back," I said.

After hanging up, it dawned on me that it must not be a column I had written. It had to be the *Milwaukee Magazine* article, but that didn't make sense because all my remarks had been off the record.

I rushed to the local book store. No copies there, but ran into a friend who remarked on the article. She had a copy at home.

The magazine article was a character assassination of Smith. Many other sources ripped him personally. Knoll quoted me at length. Worse, her editor, Bruce Murphy, used my headshot — the only photo in the article. Further, he used a partial quote from me as a sub-headline, starting with an ellipsis: "... they were in the Dark Ages."

What I had said in context was: "In terms of executive and management development, they (JCI) were in the dark ages." This was a narrow comment, not the broad slam the sub-head conveyed. My comments were strictly about the financial mistakes, not about his character.

I called Knoll, who said she had "forgotten" about the promise of confidentiality.

"No way you would have forgotten," I said. She faked an apology, but the damage was done.

I loved writing the Sunday column, even if it paid only $35 apiece (journalists always get screwed on pay). It gave me a Sunday pulpit to address one million readers, and the column was well received across the state.

I called Murphy, who had edited the piece and asked him, "How could you run those quotes? You, a seasoned journalist, must have known they were privileged. I write a column in the *Journal Sentinel.*"

He played dumb.

I called Kaiser back and told him I had been burned by two rogue journalists. He stuck to his decision.

"Did this come from the 4th floor?" I asked. That was Journal Communications headquarters where Smith had his office.

"No," he lied "It was my call."

So, here we have it — a double-barreled violation of journalism ethics:

- Knoll and Murphy outed a confidential source. I had never known a reporter to burn a source in my three decades in the news game.

- Kaiser breached the hallowed wall between the newsroom and the newspaper's business office. He was, at a minimum, sucking up to Smith, his boss, because no one ever challenged my comments on a factual or analytical basis. I had not been part of the magazine's personal attack on Smith, only on his mismanagement. I was accurate and Kaiser knew it. Further, I was going to bat for his people. At a maximum, he was following Smith's direct or indirect order.

I took to calling him "Marty Kisser," as in ass-kisser, in my recounts of my termination.

I tried to engage the Center of Journalism Ethics at UW-Madison on the two issues. They passed, preferring to deal with abstractions rather than real cases.

The loss of my bully pulpit on Sundays was a gut punch to my standing as a professional Wisconsin journalist. I tried to take it in stride, but it really hurt. I took the Knoll-Murphy ethics violations to Joel Quadracci, publisher of the magazine. He tried to duck the issue, but I insisted:

"Joel, this rises to board level in terms of seriousness." His corporate attorney, a friend, took my side.

Joel called back to say that Knoll would no longer be reporting for the magazine. She was demoted to menial writing chores.

Not long afterward, Murphy was fired.

Murphy called me to complain, saying he was only the editor, not the writer.

"Bruce, it happened on your watch," I replied. "You wrote the headlines."

My mistake was trusting Knoll. Had I checked her out, I would have learned that she was an unreliable reporter who liked to do hatchet jobs. I had always liked and respected print news people; I had never been burned or burned a source. That led me to let my guard down. Never again.

There was a happy ending of sorts. Not having the demands of a regular 750-word weekly column gave me the time to start a blog called "Straight Talk from the Heartland" at www.johntorinus.com. And it gave me the time to write two published books on reforms of the broken business model for the delivery of health care in America.

The two books sold more than 25,000 copies.

Even better, the books got me onto the national speaking circuit. It was another career of sorts. I gave more than 30 speeches to audiences large and small and able to spread the word on concepts for taming out-of-control costs in U.S. health care.

Serendipitously, I finally had figured out how to make decent money as a journalist. It wasn't the $1.50 royalty per book. My speaker's bureau set my fee at $12,500, and I gave a couple per month for a three-year run. My last keynote address went for $15,000.

Years after my termination, Murphy started running my columns in his on-line publication called *Urban Milwaukee*.

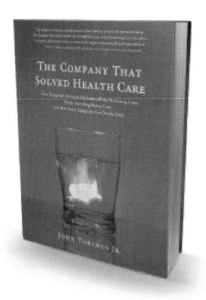
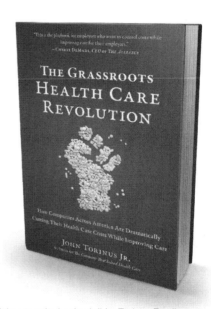

As day-to-day journalism faded from my life, I had time to write books. I did a Torinus Family History and two books on health care reform from the perspective of a payer. My company innovates on better delivery of care for our employees and their families. By helping to manage care and changing behaviors, each family saved more than $2,000 per year.

11. A Sayonara Gig in the Newsroom

EDITORIAL POSTSCRIPT

The old world of business and newspapering had been relatively stable during the 20th century, but all that changed in the age of the Internet. I was lucky to have left the print journalism business when I did. It forced me to reinvent myself. I ended up with seven distinct chapters in my career and I loved each challenge.

Most crops in the United States are cut with "sickle sections," sharp steel blades mounted on a bar that oscillates. Kondex became a major producer of a wide spectrum of cutting parts.

From an old pickle factory, Kondex grew into a modern plant of 155,000 square feet, in Lomira, Wisconsin. It became the largest producer of industrial and agricultural blades in the world.

CHAPTER 12

Back to Manufacturing:
INTO ANGEL INVESTING

Manufacturing came calling in the 1970s while I was still running the *West Bend Daily News*, taking me back to my maternal roots, the Bambeneks and Peerless Chain Company. I needed to make some money outside of Post Corp, which was paying me less than $20,000 a year as editor and general manager. I was game for a gamble on a start-up, for what came to be known as angel investing.

In that era, entrepreneurs had almost no place to go to raise capital for their new ventures except friends and family. That was the way it was for the launch of Kondex Corp.

Jim Wessing, a young purchasing agent at the Gehl Company in West Bend, Wisconsin, and Ben Braunberger, a Gehl engineer, had become aware of the acute shortage of sources for sickle sections, the triangular blades that are on the cutting front end of most agricultural harvesting machines. All the American suppliers had dropped out of the business, so Gehl was forced to fly in blades from Germany. It was a long, unreliable supply chain.

Further, Braunberger had come up with a better idea for putting the serrated teeth into the hard steel triangular blades. Instead of chiseling each tooth one by one, he proposed to coin them in a single stroke of a stamping press. It was no simple task as the 1080 steel is very hard. The stamping would curl the edge of the triangle, and he would then grind the underside flat, thus producing a very sharp, serrated edge.

The two would-be entrepreneurs had no money, and they couldn't raise capital. For help, they went to Philip Eckert, a local lawyer, Notre Dame grad and my best friend at the time. He struck out trying to raise the $500,000 Ben and Jim were looking for. So, Phil came to me looking for a way to launch the company. I suggested we boot strap it.

Phil and I each scratched together $13,000 and convinced a friend, Bob Tews, owner of a cement company, to put in $13,000. We had a paltry $39,000 in capital, but we thought we could make up for it with sweat equity. Ben and Jim were to run the company and I was to have the role of chairman. It was to become much more than that.

We bought an old stamping machine for peanuts and got my bank to give us a lease of $200,000 on an old grinder. We rented 10,000 square feet of space in a vacated, old Aunt Nellie's pickle factory in nearby Lomira for $1 per square foot. The founders went out on weekends to help rehabilitate the factory. It had open drains in the concrete floor that had been used for pickling juices, which we used for grinding fluids. We stripped old wires and conduits from the walls to hook up our machines.

Early on, we used a chiseling machine to put in the teeth one by one as Ben worked to bring the coining process on line. That technology development, not surprisingly, took far longer than planned. The 1080 steel proved exceedingly tough to coin.

As with all start-ups, early customers were hard to come by. But we finally got going with Allis Chalmers for its gleaners and later Gehl for its forage harvesters.

By then, though, we were out of cash, with no place to go for more. Ben, who had the title of president, turned out to be a good engineer, but a blockhead when it came to business. He and Jim started fighting, mainly over Ben's insistence on long runs. We were building to stock the warehouse with finished goods instead of building for order and quick cash return. We had eight million blades in inventory.

As a result, the company was going down. I had to step in as general manager. My first decision was to separate the two men, telling them not to talk to each other, to communicate only through me.

The second project was to develop real financials. We were losing money, but the financial reporting was suspect because the inventory accounting was a mess. The only way I could get a fix on inventory levels and values was a physical count at the end of each month. In my first six months, I asked my wife Pati and my two young boys to go to the warehouse on the weekend and help me with a physical count of pallets of blades. They would return home with cuts from the sharp blades.

Wessing and I did some quick cost accounting and found we were losing money on our main product, the blades, but making nice profits on the ancillary products. We had to pivot.

Wessing proved to be a good businessman. We moved into manufacture and assembly of whole sickle bars, some 30 feet long. We sourced the forged heads for each end of the bars. A company called Res Manufacturing helped us develop coining for the two-pronged blades at the end of the bars.

It was a gritty turn-around, with our bank and its regulators breathing down our necks, but by the end of 18 months, we were doing almost $2 million in business and were turning a profit of about $200,000.

That's when the ownership troubles began. Bob Tews had panicked and insisted on selling his shares back to the company. The four remaining partners each had 25 percent. Phil had promised me his vote in all matters as part of the deal for agreeing to take over as GM to turn the company around. So, even with Jim and Ben estranged, I always could count on three of the four votes on the board. It was a verbal arrangement with a best friend. Not getting our deal in writing proved to be a big mistake on my part.

Wessing and I worked well together and the company found its bearings. The company was just lifting off, heading for higher sales, earnings and valuations. Most of the stumps had been pulled and the business was shaping up. We were at an acceleration point after years of bootstrapping.

It was at that point that my best friend double-crossed me. Without telling me, he went behind my back and convinced the estranged twosome to sell the company. Phil had become an alcoholic of the binge-drinking sort. He disappeared on his binges, crashed his car several times, and lived high, sending his four children to private schools. He was desperate for cash. His promise of voting with me forever evaporated with his short-term cash needs.

Eckert started a process to sell the company. I objected, but could not convince the other two to stay the course.

Given that reality and having no capital of my own, I went to the Moon family, who owned Res and another metal bending company. I wanted the company to end up in good hands. We sold for a very low-ball offer of $800,000, not much for years of risk-taking and enormous effort.

The Moons kept Ben as a contract engineer and eventually made Wessing president. They added much-needed capital. Kondex became a $60 million company and the global leader in the manufacture of cutting mechanisms. It employs several hundred people in a modern factory on Hwy. 41 outside of Lomira, about two miles from Aunt Nellie's. I was always extremely proud of its success.

In retrospect, I should have had more confidence in myself and the company. I should have begged and borrowed enough capital to buy out all three partners, at least enough to buy out Eckert.

12. Back to Manufacturing

After the sale, I went to Eckert's law office and told him we were finished as friends. We remained civil, but seldom saw each other. He tried to renew our friendship several times. Within a few years, he was pushed out of the law firm and moved out of town. Never saw him again.

EDITORIAL POSTSCRIPT

The lessons I learned in the Kondex start-up, my mistakes, served me well. I was determined to have 51 percent control of any future venture into which I poured my life. I got 50 percent of the Serigraph buyout with a clause that would get me to 51 percent in a year or so. There were no mixed messages at Serigraph. I called the shots on tough issues when consensus could not be reached. My advice to many entrepreneurs: keep a controlling interest in the corporation. Have the confidence in yourself to be the captain of the ship.

Serigraph built a 160,000-square-foot headquarters in 1994 to serve as headquarters and factory. The modern factory proved to be a game-changer.

SPIDERWORT

COMPASS PLANT

BUTTERFLY WEED

As part of Serigraph's green strategy, which made it an environmental leader in Wisconsin, the company headquarters are surrounded by native prairie plants that attract birds and insects. A pond in the middle of the prairie collects sediment before it runs into the Milwaukee River.

CHAPTER 13

A Leveraged Buyout of Serigraph:
SCAR TISSUE PAID OFF

After 20 years of managing newsrooms, writing two to three columns per week, having a grand time as a local pundit, interacting with countless interesting people, it was time in 1987 to get out of the playpen.

I turned 50 in 1987 and was making $50,000 per year as business editor and columnist. That was the highest pay for any journalist in the *Sentinel* newsroom who was actually writing. Most editors stop writing once they move up. It's easy to duck writing, because it's hard work. I had a family to support, meager savings, and it would be at least five years before top management at the parent Journal Communications or either of its two Milwaukee papers turned over.

I might have had a shot then at an editorship or publisher, the position toward which I had pegged my career. The CEO and president of Journal Communications had asked me to head a strategic planning team to make a recommendation on whether the two Saturday papers, both anemic in terms of advertising, should be merged. It was an extraordinary exercise. The corporation had never done any long-range planning, perhaps not surprising for a monopoly that had enjoyed clear sailing for decades. The complex Saturday exercise involved analysis of all sides of the newspapers' business.

After four months of work, my positive recommendation for merger of the Saturday papers made it through the management council and board of trustees, but got lost in company politics after I left. The exercise turned out to be a precursor for full merger of the two dailies five years later.

I wish I could say I saw the pending impact of the Internet on the fortunes of newspapers as a factor in my decision to abandon my chosen career. Like most in the industry, I didn't fully understand the tsunami that would drown the industry not too far down the road. My decision to get out of newspapering was more luck than prescience.

With years as a division manager at Post, a small leveraged buyout at Menominee Publishing behind me, along with a turn-around at Kondex Corp., I thought I had the scar tissue to buy a company. I had learned, I hoped, from plenty of mistakes.

The early 1980s had seen a fever pitch of highly leveraged transactions (HLTs in bank regulatory lingo), where acquirers would pay handsome prices, load the companies with debt, pull out their equity investment as soon as possible, and then take their chances on the company making it. About half of the HLTs didn't make it. They used the bankruptcy laws to bail out.

But the half that did make it made huge returns on equity.

I had watched hot-shot George Gillett use leverage to buy Post Corp. and a young Yale grad do the same to buy my grandfa-ther's company, Peerless Chain. I had made a run in the early 1980s to use debt to buy those properties, but family dynamics wouldn't let me in the door in either case.

I thought, "If they could pull off a leveraged deal, why not me?"

On top of that, I had been editing and writing for years about the private equity firms (PEs) buying family companies with debt. Believe it or not, they would literally buy a company with ten cents in equity down on the dollar. There were plenty of willing lenders for the 90 cents. Later in 1987, that house of cards would come crashing down in the famous savings-and-loan crisis. Most of the shaky loans that caused the 1987 recession were real estate related, but some were for shaky business buyouts.

THE SCOURGE OF LEVERAGE

The failure of the government and political leaders to regulate leverage would come back to bite the U.S. economy again in 2007 in the Great Recession. Indeed, they had recklessly encouraged leverage in the cause of promoting home ownership. There were all kinds of government-backed schemes, mortgages with low or no down payments. There were even negative loans where the value of the mortgage debt exceeded 100 percent of the value of the property. Credit ratings for mortgage applicants were falsified or disregarded.

Investment banks on Wall Street were leveraged 30 to 1, far higher than my high 10-1 for Serigraph. No wonder some toppled in 2008. The survivors had to be bailed out as too big to fail.

Their biggest crime against the American economy was to package the sick loans into securities with phony positive credit ratings.

(Note that business journalists, including me, didn't see the scam until after it happened.)

The Federal Reserve has long regulated interest rates and money supply, but has generally turned a blind eye to levels of leverage across the economy.

A Yale economist, John Geanakoplos, made that case to my class at our 50th reunion in New Haven in 2009 and said he had made the same case for regulating leverage to the head of the Fed, Ben Bernanke, to no avail.

I wrote a good number of columns and blogs to promote the regulation of leverage, ala Geanakoplos. I figured he would get a Nobel Prize one day.

In early 1987, before the crash, the window to do an HLT was still open as I started looking for deal. Having covered business across the state for four years, I had ideas on where to look.

I already had one line in the water. I had called Alfred Ramsthal, founder and owner of Serigraph Sales and Manufacturing Co. in my hometown of West Bend, expressing an interest in buying his company if he ever chose to sell. Al, 79, had no heirs who he felt could take over. I knew about the company from having served on the board of its local bank. Though frail, Al said he wasn't ready to sell the company. Executives I knew at Serigraph confirmed that it was not on the market.

My second instinct was to call Sentry, where a flamboyant CEO, John Joanis, was going to step down. He had gone on an acquisition spree to diversify the company beyond insurance. He acquired manufacturing companies, built a world-class golf course in Stevens Point and bought a string of 14 radio stations.

I calculated that his successor, an actuary, would prune Sentry back to its base business of property and casualty insurance. I called a senior executive I knew and asked if Sentry wanted to sell its string of small radio stations. His initial response was, "No." But my instincts were right. He called back the next day and said, "Yes."

There was one very sticky wicket during all the negotiations. I was doing all this on the side while running the business news desk for the *Sentinel*. The potential conflict of interest was obvious. I didn't feel it was necessary to tell my boss, Bob Wills, what I was doing, because there was no deal yet. I was just exploring. But I did steer clear of publishing any stories, positive or negative, about Sentry Insurance during those weeks. (A scrupulous person could argue that, ethically, I should have resigned before wheeling and dealing.)

Without much money in my pockets, I made an offer for $8 million for the radio stations, figuring I could raise the capital at that price. Sentry countered at $10 million, and the gap was more than I wanted to bridge. So I walked from the deal and they sold to another buyer.

Early that summer, I was sitting on the business news desk and a short news release crossed my desk stating that Serigraph Sales and Mfg. Company had been sold to the Laird Group, a private equity firm out of London. I think my response was something like "SHEET!" I had missed the deal I had been tracking for several years.

But deals sometimes go awry on the way to the altar and I knew that "Alfie" — as Ramsthal was called — was a prickly, mercurial character.

I called my executive friends at the company to ask what had happened. They knew nothing about the pending deal. Alfie and his son Jimmy had not confided in them one whit.

So I called Mr. Ramsthal a couple of days later and asked if he would make me an alternate buyer if the Laird deal didn't get done. I played the local note that the company could stay locally owned if my "group," then non-existent, were to purchase Serigraph. He agreed to make me a backup.

A month went by, and I heard from one of my insider friends that the New York lawyers for Laird had managed to turn off Alfie. They had screwed the deal. I called Mr. Ramsthal and asked if would entertain a bid from me. He said he would.

He gave me the financials. The company was doing $40 million in sales and after many lackluster years had recorded a decent year in 1986 with $2 million in net income. It was a good point for him to sell, and it was a good time for me to buy.

At 12 times after-tax earnings, the prevailing price-earnings ratio at the time, it was going to be about a $24 million deal. With fees, it ended up at $28 million.

My wife Pati and I took Alfie and his wife Elsie to dinner at the "The Painted Lady" restaurant in Newburg, and we had to help him up the stairs. They were both frail. Pati and I were both careful to not hit any of Alfie's hot buttons. Even though he was not a sentimental man, I think he liked us and liked keeping ownership of the company local. We were on our way to a deal.

Of course, I didn't have the money to follow through. I was making journalist pay, $50,000 a year. I needed to raise the capital.

I had about $250,000 in reserves and figured I could personally borrow another $250,000. I called Mom, who, with my help, had just gotten $2 million out of the sale of Peerless Chain Co. She did not equivocate for an instant. She trusted me. I would carry that vote of confidence in my mind for all of my days. She lent me another $200,000 and invested $100,000. Brothers Tom and Mark, with whom I had worked at Menominee Publishing, each put in $50,000, bringing me to $900,000. I raised another $100,000 from friends.

So, I had $1 million to put into a $28 million deal.

My sons Sean and Dan, both teenagers, would ask me every night what the odds were of getting the deal done. I walked them through each step. It was a learning episode. They absorbed the ins and outs of deal making. Sean later became CEO and Dan a director of the company.

Next step was to make a case for raising another $1.5 million in equity and $25.5 million in debt.

I called brother Tom, a Phi Beta Kappa graduate of Dartmouth in economics and a seasoned editor, for help. He came to West Bend and spent two weeks at my house writing the business plan. I pitched in before and after work and weekends.

My first stop with our home-brewed business plan in hand was Dick Fischer, an executive at Robert W. Baird & Co., a regional investment banking house. Baird must have liked the business plan, because it offered to do the financing. Fisher proposed that I receive ten percent of the deal. I diplomatically told him to put his offer where the sun doesn't shine. I wanted 51 percent. No more split control like I had suffered through at Kondex.

My second stop was Dudley Godfrey, the highly respected head of the mid-size business law firm, Godfrey & Kahn S.C. in Milwaukee. I had interviewed him several times when I was business editor and I knew his firm did some "merchant bank-ing," where members of the firm invested in deals they were working. Dudley, who was to become my business godfather, was superb. He offered me 50 percent, and we had a deal. As part of it, he gave me a path to 51 percent if the company hit certain milestones under my leadership.

Dudley's first step was to call Morgan Stanley, the power-house New York investment banking firm. It agreed to help, even though the deal was too small for them.

Frank Sica, a Morgan partner, called Ramsthal and told him that Morgan was backing Torinus. That got me to the front of the bidding pack. Morgan never did put any money in the small deal, but Sica put in $250,000 of his own money. He got it back three times over when he made an exit two years later. He was the first investor to exit and redeeming his shares gave me control.

Dudley agreed to go on my board for two years and stayed for 22. He was invaluable. When he died, I was up north skiing at our cabin. I drove seven hours through a fierce blizzard to get to his services in Milwaukee. Godfrey & Kahn became our perpetual law firm.

The two junior lawyers on the deal were Andy Ziegler, who went on to found the Artisan Funds and become a billionaire, and John Peterson, who went on to head a boutique investment banking company in Milwaukee. With Dudley's connections, Peterson crafted a deal that raised another $1.5 million in equity from old money in Milwaukee, for a total of $2.5 million in equity. Those who contended that the old money in Milwaukee was too conservative were wrong.

We borrowed the remaining $25.5 million from three sources, the state pension fund, Prudential Insurance and Bank One. The leverage was ten to one.

My metaphor for highly leveraged transactions is that they are a high wire act. You look spectacular up there on the wire, but one misstep and you are the remains of an abrupt plummet to earth. Half of the leveraged buyouts of that era didn't make it.

The deal closed Sept. 1, 1987. I told Bob Wills several weeks earlier that I would be leaving The *Sentinel* and he begged me to stay on for six more weeks, which I did. My run as an editor and columnist had gone well. I left on good terms.

Serigraph had a lot going for it, particularly some proprietary technology and an effective sales operation. It had pioneered interstation ultraviolet curing for lithographic presses and that breakthrough provided a quality and productivity edge with customers like McDonald's for its in-store advertising. Its buyer fancied himself a cutting-edge print guru. He wanted his French fries to look edible and irresistible on the menu display. Serigraph rode that technology for a decade before other printers caught up.

I used that foothold in technological innovation as a base for an innovation strategy, similar to what Harry Quadracci deployed to build QuadGraphics into a leader of the print world. Harry was a master innovator, so I always kept track of what he was doing. He used technology in the ultimate commodity business, printing magazines, to win a productivity edge. That cost-saving edge allowed him to win big contracts with the likes of *Time* and *Playboy*. Those contracts allowed him to obtain leases from banks for monster presses at $3 million or more. He had created a powerful circular dynamic, starting with technology.

Essentially, my team at Serigraph plagiarized that innovation strategy. We had one chemist and one quality engineer at the outset. We began a program to add a couple more every year.

But, first, we had to improve the company's cash flow so we could handle the debt service required by 10-1 leverage.

As good as Serigraph was in sales and innovation, it was behind the curve on manufacturing, strategy, professional

John and Molly Torinus at Serigraph headquarters in West Bend, Wisconsin.

management and teamwork. Those were areas where I had a lot of experience.

My first day on the job was a doozie. Al and Jim Ramsthal, his son who had the title of president, opened all the mail, including personal mail, every morning. There were two huge bins of mail, so it took them most of the morning.

Then they would listen in on employee telephone conversations in the afternoon, unbeknownst to the callers. It was quasi legal because they had a sticker on each phone saying it were subject to monitoring. Sometimes they would chew out an employee based on what they heard, even fire them. These were their ways of staying in control. It was top-down management by intimidation.

Day one, I ripped out the phone monitoring system and delegated the sorting of the mail. Jimmy told me I was making a big mistake.

Day three, I ended the booze culture. I went to lunch at the Coachman House, a local watering hole, on day two and found about 15 Serigraphers drinking their lunch. The next day, I prohibited drinking during working hours. It was a far piece from the occasional three-martini lunches I had encountered when I broke into the business world at Post Corporation.

I convinced most of the seasoned managers to stay on, but started immediately to recruit and promote young, talented people. Going through the personnel files, I found a guy named Mike Palm, who was running the tool room. He had an MBA from DePaul. I went back to the tool room to meet him and asked him if he would take on more responsibility. He had put himself through school as a master tool-and-die maker. He turned me down. "I like the tool room." It took me six months to convince him to run industrial engineering. He went on to become COO of the company. We became life-long friends, sharing biking and skiing activities.

13. A Leveraged Buyout of Serigraph

We adopted an engagement philosophy for all co-workers with the mantra: "Help Run Your Company." We adopted lean disciplines and a heavy dose of profit sharing.

It worked and we quickly doubled operating profits. That made the leverage manageable. And it made stock buybacks possible throughout the 1990s. The state investment board, for example, got out with a 41 percent annual rate of return.

I always wanted my investors to get a great return, so I could refer future investors to them. I felt the same way about the Ramsthal family, the sellers. Bob Ramsthal, confined to a wheelchair, stayed on at Serigraph for a nice career running our telecommunications.

By the time the company reached the 2000s, much had been accomplished:

Most of the stock of outside investors had been redeemed through a big round of new debt in 1998. That left only the G&K lawyers, with about 17 percent of the company, my siblings with 16 percent, and a couple dozen co-workers who had purchased shares. They were my patient investors.

We had grown to $158 million in sales at our high point, thanks in part to a rush of business in "tazos," a premium placed in snack food bags all over Latin and South America, particularly in Mexico. We made literally billions of them at about a penny apiece.

We had become an international company, with two businesses in Mexico, two plants in China and a joint venture in Bangalore, India. In an episode of arrogance, son Sean and I declared: "If you are not in global manufacturing, you are not in manufacturing." During and after the Great Recession, we had to undo that global strategy to concentrate on North America.

On the innovation side, we pioneered in-mold decorating (IMD), which involved putting a formed graphic inside an injection molding machine to come out with a fused decorative part. It carried the company for years, much as interstation UV curing had earlier.

We developed a culture where people could derive satisfaction from their work lives, where they respected each other and had some fun on the job. It became an interdependent community. We de-managed, meaning decisions were made at the lowest level possible. We have gone deep into a lean discipline journey that centers on engaging every employee every day in continuous improvement, knowing we would never get all the way there.

We survived three recessions, including the Great Recession of 2008 to 2010 that almost took the company down. Sales collapsed. We made the painful but existentially necessary cost reductions. Our long-time policy of layoffs only as a last resort had to go. We reduced ranks as humanely as possible. We went from 873 co-workers to 410 at the low point. In the end, we came out a leaner, more solid company.

I ran the company as CEO and Chairman from the acquisition date in 1987 until I turned 70 in 2007. I enjoyed it all. It was the best gig I ever had, though I loved journalism, too.

It wasn't automatic that my oldest son Sean (John III) would take over. He was too young, but he made himself ready. He rotated through every tough job in the company and went to graduate school weekends and nights to earn two master's degrees in business and information technology. He embraced tough assessments of his development from experts like the Center for Creative Leadership, which slices and dices personalities and performance in an unblinking way.

He had earned the role of Chief Operating Officer by 2007, after having served as Chief Information Officer, division manager of our troubled Mexican operations and our struggling Specialty Division on his return to the states. Even though he was only 37, he and I agreed that he was ready to take over as CEO. I wasn't quite ready to step aside, having been blessed with good health, but Sean was ready.

We hired a human resources psychologist to help us through the transition. We wanted to get our roles straight, so there would be no conflict about who was doing what with him as CEO and me as Chairman of the Board. We had hired psychologists with business expertise twice before to make sure we were aligned, once when Sean came into the company at age 24, and again about a decade later to make sure his development as an executive was on track.

A very bright man with a quick mind, Sean was often the first in the room with the answer. But by 2007, he had learned from hard knocks in business to stay in the question and listen hard to other people with ideas on the issue of the day. We both had come to know that if you are the smartest person in the room, you are in big trouble. A dialogue with other smart people always yields a better answer.

With the help of the consultant, we divided our roles. I took external roles, like government and public relations, along with shareholder and board relations. I kept oversight of health care and retirement benefits. Sean took all the core functions.

There was one wrinkle. I asked to keep the leadership of our lean journey, because I loved the factory and operations. But it proved to have too much crossover into what Sean was trying to accomplish. So, six months down the road, he asked to take over our lean initiative. I saw the conflict and agreed. He later expanded that into a major strategy for the company.

Sean wanted the corner office on executive row and my brothers advised me to give it up. Sean had a nice office built for me on the other end of the building. I enjoyed going to work there every day and mixing with our professional staff.

Sean's maturation as a tough-minded executive was soon tested to the max.

The Great Recession, caused by the nation's genius leaders on Wall Street and inside the beltway in the nation's capitol, kicked in late in 2007, just months after Sean moved into the CEO chair. It was an earthquake that became a tsunami. In some ways, it was a worse catastrophe than the Great Depression. Essentially, the nation, especially the housing and mortgage markets, were allowed by the politicos and regulators to become grossly over-leveraged. That bubble burst, and the collateral damage was deep and wide.

Some sectors like banking, real estate and capital goods were slammed more than others. Serigraph sells graphics to the durable goods industry, more specifically to the discretionary durable goods producers, and that sector was devastated. Mercury engine sales went off 60 percent; car sales were down 40 percent; recreational vehicles went into hibernation. Our overall sales fell off about 40 percent at the low point in 2009.

I had been through storms and recessions before and Sean had done turn-arounds. We conferred daily. We knew what we had to do: damage control. We threw out the strategic plan that was based on stability and growth and managed with one objective: stay positive each month on cash flow.

Conventional business wisdom is that if you have to make personnel cuts, do it once and get it over with. But we couldn't find bottom for the sales fall-off. We ended up making four painful rounds of cuts.

BMO Harris Bank put us into default on our $18 million in loans and assigned us to its tough workout team. Sean negotiated more than a dozen loan forbearance extensions. It took until 2014 to get a five-year extension of our line of credit. Banks are never your friends, but BMO hung in there with us — mainly because we did the necessary emergency surgery and were always totally straight with them. Both gave us credibility. We almost lost the company, but we survived.

We also had made it a rule to always be straight with our co-workers, good times or bad, and it paid off. They hung in with us, too, even when we cut wages by five percent, laid off their friends and family members, and eliminated their 401(k) retirement match.

We tried to do our staff reductions with the utmost of care. We used attrition, moved people into open roles, offered attractive early retirement packages, limited terminations within a family and paid for outplacement services for as long as it took for people to find a new job. Only a few were bitter, and most understood that the company had to survive. Several who lost their jobs came to my office to tell me "thanks" for having been able to work at the company. I couldn't believe their goodwill.

Before it was over, we had closed both our China plants, sold our Mexican point-of-purchase company and had cut every expense item, including pet R&D projects.

One of our principles was that we kept our best performers. That meant production did not suffer proportionally to the cuts. Our productivity per employee rose. We came out of the crash a smaller but leaner organization. That was a critical factor in weathering the storm.

Diversification also helped, since the Specialty Division that sold to quick-service restaurants suffered less impact than our Industrial Graphics Division. It had profitable years, as did Carvel, our POP business in Mexico, when we badly needed them.

I kept a tally of auto parts companies that went under. It topped 70. Among them were Visteon and Delphi, major auto parts suppliers that were big customers of ours. GM and Chrysler also went into bankruptcy reorganization.

Were we lucky to survive? Yes and no. Mainly, it was hard-nosed dealing with reality that kept us afloat. I told Sean I had his back as he made many tough calls. He had enough stress without my second-guessing him. He proved to be an excellent downside manager.

An example was Visteon, a supplier to Ford. We knew they were going into Chapter 11 bankruptcy while owing us about a million dollars. We couldn't take that hit. Sean pored over their general services contract and found it was about to expire at the end of calendar 2009.

He waited until then and informed Visteon it either had to pay its arrearage or we would stop shipping parts. They refused, took us to court and won a temporary restraining order (TRO) to force us to continue to supply parts. We shipped the 60 days that the TRO required and then went back to the judge to inform him Visteon still was not paying. He ordered Visteon to pay us forthwith. Our CFO got on a chartered plane to fly to Michigan to pick up the check for fear they would go bankrupt any hour. A wire transfer of $600,000 came through while he was in the air over Lake Michigan bound for Ann Arbor and the plane turned around to return to West Bend.

About two weeks later, Visteon went into Chapter 11 reorganization. Our receivable would have been flushed. That was just one of many tough calls that saved Serigraph from a similar fate.

Sean and I developed a closer working relationship amidst the trauma. It prevailed from then on. I didn't get much involved in the operations of the business, but he engaged me in all the big stuff. We conferred several times a week. I was his ultimate sounding board. Being outside the daily fray, I could offer a slant on his big issues. From my perspective it worked great, even though we didn't always agree. We have quite different personalities and some differences in management styles.

We came out of the Great Recession with three major goals: we wanted to sharply reduce the debt, so we could more easily weather future storms; we wanted to buy out our remaining investors, mainly my siblings and Godfrey & Kahn attorneys; and we wanted to engage all our co-workers in an uber-lean enterprise.

By the end of 2016, we had reduced out debt to about $13 million, still more than we wanted, but manageable even with so-so cash flows. We set a goal of being debt-free in three years, barring any major expeditions.

My obsession was to buy back the stock of all remaining investors, including shares held by my family and our law firm. They had been patient investors for 28 years. Only brother Mark had taken any major dollars out by selling shares back to the company. I felt a moral obligation to give them a decent return on their investment in me.

By 2013, my siblings were at or near retirement and feeling financial pressure. Perhaps in anticipation of a major payout from Serigraph, they had not planned well for their later years. Even though we were still in recovery mode and under bank constraints, Mark, who had suffered a stroke and other physical problems, started pushing hard for an exit. He rallied the other siblings, hired an attorney/CPA, and took his needs to the board, where he was a director.

He had taken Tom's seat on the board. Tom better understood the tenuous condition of the company and served to keep the siblings apprised of what was possible and what was not.

All during the 28 years of our mutual ownership, I had convened and run a family council to keep communication lines open. It worked beautifully for 26 years.

I did get a stream of tough letters from several relatives and one close friend whom I had included in the initial deal. It was disappointing, to say the least.

But we had no options that worked for buyer and seller. I explored them all. Finally, in 2015, we caught a break. Our majority partners in a joint venture in Bangalore, India decided to retire and sell our joint venture, SJS. They had made one earlier run at selling, but this time they were determined. We owned 26 percent of SJS.

Sean agreed that I would take the point from our end, because he had strained relations with Sivakumar, CEO of SJS, and I had experience with deals. I like to think that I helped Siva and his partner Srini avoid the mistakes that had cratered their earlier attempt at a sale.

SJS had done spectacularly well, with only limited synergistic help from Serigraph. From a $4 million company when we invested, it had grown to $26 million in revenues and had incredible cash flow margins north of 25 percent. It was worth a lot of money.

We got the deal done, a sale to an Indian private equity company based in Singapore. It got done amidst a tangle of Indian bureaucracy that makes U.S. agencies look like a walk in the park. After taxes and fees, we took home a check of $7.5 million. We had invested $4.7 million back in 2007. It was a nice gain that would have been doubled if the Indian rupee had not fallen off by half against the dollar over the eight years.

It was nice to have a winner after losses on our two start-up plants in China and mixed results in the POP business in Mexico. We retained our Industrial Graphics plant in Querétaro, Mexico, and it continued to be a contributor. From Mexico, we believed we could compete effectively with Asian suppliers on labor-intensive jobs going forward. That included competition from the new owners of SJS.

Sean and I had developed a deep sense of humility. Our strategy of being a thoroughly global supplier had been a mixed success at best. We thought we could pull it off. Our people logged many thousands of air miles to support our global ambitions; Sean was a platinum flyer. But the customers who insisted we support them in China and India proved slippery. Unfortunately, we could not put together permanent local management teams. We might have kept those bets going, but the recession ruled out any adventures that were not positive for cash flow. Of necessity, we retreated to North America.

BUYING OUT FAMILY AND FRIENDS

The proceeds from India gave us the cash to launch a tender offer for the outside shares. Dec. 1, 2015 was a happy day for me and my long-patient investors. Most had invested in 1987 at $50 per share or its equivalent. The tender was for $925 per share.

There was a good deal of back-and-forth about the price. Some family members wanted $1,000 to $1,200 per share, remembering that the stock had reached $1,600 in the late 1990s when all systems were go. Sean and I recalled 2009, when the stock was worth zero, and a few years back when appraisals put minority shares at $736.

Tom and I asked Pat Egan, a family friend who had run a similar sized family business and had bought out siblings, to mediate. He did a great job of getting my siblings to deal with the realities of 2015.

Our board of directors, especially the five outside directors, made the final call at $925.

On an investment of $67,000 each, Tom got a check for about $1.2 million; Maryclaire, Mark's widow, got $900,000 on top of the $450,000 they had pulled out earlier. My other siblings got about $300,000 each on the $17,000 that Mother had invested on their behalf. It was a return of about 9 percent per year over 28 years. Not bad, given the many economic convulsions in those three decades.

In the end, everyone was satisfied with the amount and the process. All outside shareholders tendered. It was the finale I had always envisioned.

That said, the buy-back of shares came at the perfect time just as they retired. Tom wryly observed that it was a good thing that the payout hadn't come earlier. The funds might have been spent.

The tender also took out employees who had invested at various junctures. Most made a decent return, but a handful had invested at higher than $925 per share. I wrote personal checks to make them whole. I also wrote a personal note to thank the G&K lawyers who had been such patient investors and supporters.

The redemption of shares launched a new era of ownership for Serigraph. The company was now owned 100 percent by me, my two sons, and trusts set up for them and future generations.

Serigraph was still leveraged, now with about $17 million in debt. But Sean and I were confident that we could manage the leverage and bring the debt down. We owned the company, but it was not without risk.

As part of our planning for the big redemption, we did sensitivity analysis. Would the company be all right if we lost our two biggest customers? The answer was that finances would be tight, but we could make it through.

13. A Leveraged Buyout of Serigraph

And, unfortunately, that's exactly what happened. For reasons largely beyond our control, we lost the Arby's and Select Comfort accounts, about ten percent of our business. It hurt, but we survived, thanks mainly to outstanding performance in our factory operations.

Per-share value dropped. My siblings and G&K lawyers had sold at a propitious point in time.

Clairvoyantly, Sean and his team had taken the deepest of dives into the lean disciplines that had been pioneered by Toyota 40 years earlier. Scrap rates dropped. Wastes of all types melted away. Deliveries improved. Quality soared as defects in products disappeared. We won customers back. That got us through the revenue slump.

Outside quality auditors made Serigraph a benchmark for other companies for management systems that aligned company goals and metrics with the efforts of each co-worker.

In addition, we made a major strategic move beyond printing of decorative parts. We moved into molding as well. Our people picked it up quickly, and we had a more complete solution for customers.

By mid-2017, we had pulled back to acceptable profitability. Debt levels dropped.

By 2018, the complexity of new parts we signed up for took us back into the swamp. We had way underpriced our biggest contract. We were back in trouble with our bank, BMO Harris. Our POP Division was doing very well, thanks to the turnaround engineered by two of our veteran managers. But our Industrial Graphics division was drowning in scrap levels as high as 35 percent on some customers. It lost a half million on both November and December. The bank, rightfully, put us in "forbearance" and we had to realign our fixed costs.

January 2019 was one of the more painful segments in my long career. We had to let 17 people go, most of them long-term employees. That included Mike Palm, our COO, who had turned 65, had 35 years of sterling service to the company, and had become one of my best friends. He had "pulled" me to a 76-mile bike ride on the year of my 76th birthday. He took early retirement with ultimate grace and thanked me for a fulfilling career as our number-two guy. We remained close friends and I was able to help him find an adjunct professor gig teaching international business at the University of Wisconsin–Milwaukee.

We used early retirement packages wherever possible.

Sean and I were determined to use those cost cuts as a platform for getting the company to high ground. Toyo Consulting picked us as one of three companies in the country to move to a more robust culture of continuous improvement.

The company was on better footing as we worked toward improved results in 2019. Mid-2019, the executive shifted gears from survival mode to growth and technology innovation.

By March 2020, we were back on solid ground. We had closed our remaining Mexican plant, because we could absorb the work in West Bend, where our productivity far exceeded what would could achieve south of the border. The productivity excellence trumped the wage differential.

Also, Sean accomplished the near-impossible. He renegotiated the contract that was killing us and won a 35 percent price increase. That was worth more than $1.5 million in profits per year.

The sun was shining on us again in early 2020, but we never got to enjoy the moment. The novel coronavirus devastated the US economy starting on March 15 of that year.

We were back into crisis management. A $4.6 million federal government loan kept us running, but the future was so uncertain that we knew draconian measures would be required next if the pandemic persisted. The loan was "forgivable" if we kept most of our jobs. Our balance sheet looked a lot better after that.

Business rebounded in 2021 and we were a solid company again, not without a lot of financial stress with our bank. We worked like our business life depended on it — and survived.

EDITORIAL POSTSCRIPT

Business is often a roller coaster. We learned the hard way that debt is a killer on the downward plunges. I would still take on major debt again for major adventures like the purchase of Serigraph, when I had much to gain and little to lose. My mistake was not raising outside capital when times were good to shed debt as fast as possible. If a company is debt-free or debt-light, it can survive most any adversity.

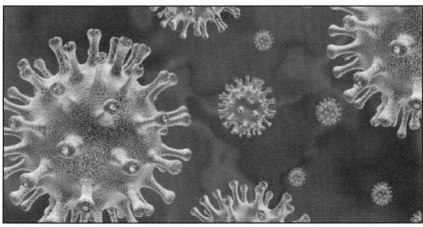

The corona virus (Covid 19), delivered a mighty blow to the world, the United States, and Serigraph in 2021. It was the company's toughest chapter ever.

The best part of owning and managing a company is the opportunity to create a healthy enterprise that is good for co-workers and their families, customers, investors, vendors in the supply chain, and the community. There are always issues, but by developing mutual respect among all stakeholders through open communication and honest dialogue, the organization becomes a positive force for all. It's a great feeling to go to work and see people collaborating as a team. Everyone wants to belong to a healthy, lively, successful team. Building a high-performance company that people want to be a part of was always my ambition in life. Despite some painful economic times and necessary adjustments, we largely accomplished that at Serigraph.

13. A Leveraged Buyout of Serigraph

To honor Serigraph's 50th anniversary in 1999, Tom Torinus, an investor and director for 20 years, wrote this tribute to the company and its people:

ABOUT SERIGRAPH

If we can run this place
to the rhythm of the human heart,
we shall.

If we can make it not a machine, not an idea, not even a system
but a breathing, beating being of a place, we shall.

If we can rely not on numbers and reports
to measure ourselves by,
but our own hearty and lusty pleasure of work together,
we shall.

If we can keep reaching higher and deeper,
higher and deeper than we ever imagined we would go,
we shall.

We have an adventure together, a great lusty adventure of
coming together each day
to create something strong and beautiful.

More than what we make together to think up together,
we are that creation.

And we will by god every day strive to savor, respect,
appreciate what we build together so well.

This wonderful thing we are.

FUELING THE INNOVATION OF WISCONSIN'S ENTREPRENEURS

Our venture fund raised about $10 million for an even dozen high-tech start-ups in Wisconsin. It led the way for other start-up funds.

BIZSTARTS
———— INSTITUTE ————
Empowerment Through Entrepreneurship

PROGRAM FORMED TO CREATE SUCCESSFUL BUSINESS OWNERS FROM UNDER SERVED COMMUNITIES

GAIN EXPERTISE, CONFIDENCE AND RESOURCES TO BUILD WEALTH OVER TIME.

ONE-ON-ONE ACCESS TO THE BEST BUSINESS MENTORS AND CONSULTANTS

BizStarts set out to create an entrepreneurial ecosystem where start-ups could go for counsel and mentorship. It helped entrepreneurs with business plans and connections to capital.

The University of Wisconsin—Milwaukee (UWM) became the second research campus in the state. As its first chairman, I watched with pride as it became a leader on patents, licenses, and start-ups.

CHAPTER 14

Jump-Starting Angel Investing:
RENAISSANCE IN THE RUST BELT

E ver since the four UW economic summits on the future of
the Wisconsin economy from 2000 to 2003, I had been
working to shift public policy in the state to an embrace
of entrepreneurs. Wisconsin had lagged the U.S. average for GDP
growth for four decades, because, in my analysis, it lacked venture capital and an entrepreneurial ecosystem.

As a Rust Belt state, Wisconsin could no longer rely on manufacturing and agri-business for job growth. Both sectors had become increasingly productive so that far fewer employees were
needed to get the work done. Less than two percent of the population is now required in farming to feed the nation and other parts
of the world. By 2030, less than five percent would be needed to
make all the products we could stuff into houses, garages, and
mini-storage units.

Ergo, our economy had to be reinvented and diversified and
it's entrepreneurial innovators who do just that.

To ratify that point, we must always bear in mind that almost
all of Wisconsin's great employers had started in the state and we
had once been an entrepreneurial state. Further, here in the
"frozen tundra," we were never good at recruiting companies
from other states and nations. The $4-billion subsidy in 2018 to
attract Foxconn, a ruthless contract manufacturer, to Racine
County turned into a major bust. We had been completely snook-
ered in what was a high-stakes political drama.

To set the foundation for a better strategy for prosperity, another activist and I created "BizStarts Milwaukee" in 2008. It was a vehicle to build a buzz for entrepreneurship and a home for mentoring start-ups in southeastern Wisconsin. It worked. Madison had a head start on forming new companies. But other incubators and venture accelerators followed our lead. They started popping up in Milwaukee and across the state.

When three other entrepreneurs and I started Kondex back in the 1970s, there was nowhere to go for advice or seed capital. It could only be a total bootstrap operation. We raised a grand total of $39,000, rewired the old Aunt Nellie's pickle factory rented at $1 per square foot per year, and used the old wiring to rewire our machines.

Once BizStarts was up and running as a support system by 2012, I decided to tackle the other gap in the state's start-up picture — the dearth of early stage capital to fund Wisconsin ventures.

There had been several pioneers who started angel groups, loose collections of individual investors who met together, but with each making an individual investment decisions. By 2015, there were more than 40 such groups across the state, but they were each doing only one or two deals per year. With two other partners, I started one of those loose-knit groups in the Milwaukee Region to test the waters.

The groups, including ours, were clunky. Each deal was like herding cats to get the members to write individual checks.

Instead, Tom Schuster, Jackie Darr and I decided we needed to create an angel fund, which we named the Wisconsin Super Angel Fund. There was none in Milwaukee. With an angel fund, the financial commitments are made up front by investors. The general partners make the calls and move fast to get deals done.

14. Jump-Starting Angel Investing

We worked more than a year to raise the fund from the "old money" in Milwaukee. In the end, we raised the $10 million from supposedly "risk-adverse" Milwaukee investors. We had honed our pitch deck and made dozens of sales calls. Our main theme was that Wisconsin was rich in intellectual property and that the Midwest, fly-over country, had been overlooked for good investments.

The 62 limited partners we landed included successful business people, five foundations and one insurance company. They were making bets to test our proposition and to propel the state.

Our other theme was that we would be looking for early exits — sales of the ventures in three to five years. (In the end, we needed more time.)

Between 2013 and 2017, we made investments in twelve deals ranging between $250,000 and $500,000.

I had made seven angel investments before starting our fund and had been in general management of three start-ups. I thought I had made every business mistake that could be made. To help us with our judgments, we created an investment committee of four highly successful business people. Despite all that scar tissue, we proceeded to make our share of new mistakes.

Our first investment was in NexVex, a company with a new business model for getting estimates for home roof repairs. It was based on actual quotes from roofers using satellite roof photos, not tape-measure estimates by the insurance claims adjusters. It never caught on with insurance companies, even though it would have saved them tons of money. Our mistake: we didn't dig deep enough with the potential customers, the property insurers. We listened to the entrepreneurs, who always have a passionate story to tell. Five years later we bailed out and arranged for a wind-down of the company from which we might recoup a few bucks.

Another misadventure that should have been a positive story was a "sweet cranberry" company. Our founder, a Wisconsin PhD in food science, had invented a way to de-acidify tart berries, instead of jamming them full of sugar like every other cranberry product on the market. Brilliant science, but he turned out to be a poor businessman. After three years of struggle and burning cash to get the manufacturing and revenue going, we finally broke through to $300,000 a month in revenue in December 2018 with sales to Walmart and Costco. We were finally running to daylight and making money.

Then came a bizarre turn of events. The company had taken a $522,000 loan from the small Community Bank of Little Chute. We were current on the loan. Then there was a CEO change at the bank and without warning, the new guy, under pressure from bank regulators, called the loan, and grabbed our cash and newly sizeable receivables. He gave us almost no time to refinance. We had to liquidate, even though we had a half million dollars in orders on the books for the next couple of months. Afraid of being sued, our fund's two representatives on the board resigned and ran for cover.

Tom Schuster and I, both turn-around veterans, drove immediately to the Menasha plant and dug in. We realized that it had just landed Costco and Walmart as customers and had become a going concern. We appealed to the bank. But we were just too late. The company was liquidated.

Lessons learned: bring in a business professional as CEO after launch to replace the visionary founder and never, ever use bank debt as capital. Banks and regulators don't have the stomach for start-ups, which are always hairy. In retrospect, we probably should have sued the bank for tanking the company.

14. Jump-Starting Angel Investing

We did have two early exits to offset the bets that didn't work out. We sold Fishidy, a social media site for anglers, to Flir Corp. for $7 million, about a two times return in three years. It was good to be in a syndicate with other smart and seasoned early stage investors. Fishidy didn't have much revenue, but it did have one million people — eyeballs — using its free site. The sale was something of a Hail Mary pass, because there were no other potential buyers. That reality caused our sale price to drop from $10 million to $7 million.

Our fund made a huge bet by using our profits from the Fishidy deal to double down on Mikkelsen Cutting Tools. Once again, the founders were visionary, came up with a great product — a large format digital cutting machine for the printing industry — and got a rudimentary plant up and running. We won product of the year in the nation's biggest printing trade show in 2017.

All that gets you to first base. While bright, neither founder was a trained engineer or business manager. It took five years to get to selling three machines a month — barely breakeven.

We repeatedly had to write checks, personal and from the fund, to cover the bi-weekly payroll. We were running on fumes. We were fighting two established incumbents, who kept telling customers that we were going under. They weren't far from wrong. Higher sales were always just around the corner.

This time, we moved more quickly. We took over the board and John Busby, a seasoned executive and one of our investors, became interim chairman and acting CEO. Finally, even he wore out. Running start-ups is a lot tougher than running the big, cash-flowing companies that John had always managed.

But John helped us get to where we got lucky. Through Rak Kumar, another board member and investor, we found a buyer who liked our technology. With Rak and me on the board, helping to babysit the Mikkelsens, Tom Schuster stepped in as interim CEO. We were holding the company together with duct tape.

This time, the local bank hung with us and pushed back on the regulators so we could keep our $750,000 line of credit.

Rak and Tom got a deal done with Gerber Technologies without a lot of strong cards to play. We got a low down payment of about $3 million, enough to pay the bank back in full, pay off our stretched-out vendors and pay off preferential senior notes that we had sold while teetering on the edge of collapse.

But we also got a three-year "earn-out," 11 percent of revenues over the next three years. We made the bet that Gerber's large, international sales force would sell many more than three machines a month. And we knew their engineers would streamline the factory operations.

About six months after the sale, we got the happy news that Gerber was selling ten machines a month. We were headed for a very profitable earn-out. Our gamble looked to be paying off. It was misplaced optimism.

The big guns at Gerber corporate decided they had better answers. They moved the factory from Wisconsin to Connecticut and screwed up the operations. That hurt sales, as did their termination of our best sales people and the two founders.

Our earn-out was in jeopardy and the Gerber execs tried to get whole by claiming $500,000 out of the escrow amount that was held back. We caved because of legal fees.

Over the three year earn-out period we did reap some modest returns, but far less than we had expected. Those returns were better than liquidating the company for lack of operating cash.

Jackie guided us to our first home run. As a director, she steered one of our startups to an "eight-bagger," an eight-time return on our initial investment. Our $4 million payout lifted our limited partners to nearly a full return of their capital. We still had four good bets on the table.

Lessons learned: the founders almost always are not capable of building a company; they almost always need to be replaced early on or buttressed with other talent, never an easy transition. They love their baby, their creation and they have a hard time dealing with the tough realities of the marketplace. Why doesn't everyone else love their baby like they do? Their blindness borders on delusion. Ergo: they do need an active board of directors, but without those passionate innovators, companies would never launch. Bless them all.

EDITORIAL POSTSCRIPT

Once again, don't use bank debt as capital in a start-up. Our MCT loan was always on the regulator watch list; we were always in default and subject to losing the loan.

And avoid earn-outs as payment. Unscrupulous buyers can always find ways to chisel money from the original deal.

As for the rest of the fund, three other of our 12 companies were also on the rocks, but we had five good bets still on the table as we entered 2020. Two were looking like big wins. We were confident that we would close the fund with a strong return for our limited partners. But, it would take longer than we had pitched.

If Tom and Jackie started another fund, based on a successful first fund, we decided they should move up a notch in the investment hierarchy. It would be a "Venture A" fund that steps in as companies achieve lift-off. The ventures would have a growing top line and some bottom line. The new fund would put in $1 million to $5 million in deals to scale up the companies to major success.

We had learned that pure start-ups are a tough investment proposition.

At the age of 84, with a bout of manageable prostate cancer on my resume, it was time to harvest our outstanding deals.

Back to the big picture in Wisconsin: from the bottom of the 50 states, we had moved up to the middle of the pack for venture investing. We were at a run rate of more than $400 million per year in early-stage investing across the state by 2019.

Where few existed in 2000, there were now start-up support organizations all over the state and on most university campuses. There still wasn't much help from state government, except for the very effective 25 percent investment tax credits. Maybe that's for the best.

I started pushing for moving the credit to 50 percent and a bright legislator introduced a bill to that effect. That would de-mark Wisconsin as the best place in the country to start a company.

Finally, our country needs to revel in the success of our entrepreneurs, even the billionaires. For equity's sake, though, tax the bejesus out of them personally on earnings above 100 times average US wages. That goes for movie stars, CEOs, athletes, and money managers as well.

Many entrepreneurs who exit their companies become very generous. One friend lives in a 1,200-square-foot duplex and he is giving away all his millions. He and his wife are very happy.

The proceeds from entrepreneurial successes need to be spread around, even beyond the benefits of new product and services and the job creation and fresh tax revenues they have created.

Stu Carlson, my one-time protégé as a young cartoonist, drew this depiction of me fighting the powerful "medical-industrial complex."

Intense, almost to a fault, talking health care costs with Governor Tommy Thompson.

CHAPTER 15

Making Policy from the Ground Up:
TAMING THE HEALTH COST BEAST

T
here are so many good fights that need to be fought. It would be fun to lead multiple lives to take on more of them.

Why, I often wondered, did so few business people and journalists get directly involved in politics or policymaking? Those professions have been my two worlds, and I have been a rare bird who engaged some of the issues of the day beyond the day-to-day job.

There's an obvious answer on the journalist side. Newspeople, bless them all, are more observers than actors on the stage. Their noses are against the windowpanes to the real world. They are forever trying to figure out and report on what's going on beyond the opaque glass.

My conclusion about business people is that they are consumed with making their companies successful. Mostly, they engage in policy and politics only when their corporate interests are directly involved, but then it's mostly to write checks to political campaigns or to sit helpfully but quietly on boards of staff-driven non-profit organizations. Their passivity is a loss. If more engaged, their problem-solving skills could be of great use in cracking through on larger public issues.

The few business people I know who did fully engage in public matters have been very effective. Most, though, take a pass on the contentious world of politics and public policy.

In truth, I never fully engaged either. I never had the guts to run for public office, even though I often was asked to do so. There were plenty of reasons to not run: time for family, the long commute to the capitols in Madison or D.C., love of journalism, the press of managing business turnarounds or start-ups, and the need to make a decent living.

I was approached twice to be in a Wisconsin governor's cabinet as secretary of the Department of Commerce, a pivotal but thankless job. I found reasons to pass, even though economic development was a major avocation for most of my adult life. Due to some prodding, I gave serious consideration to running for governor or U.S. senator in the 1990s. In the end, I always flinched, opting always to stay in the two worlds where I was comfortable—business and journalism.

Who knows if I would have been an effective politician?

In some ways, though, you can get more done in public policy on the outside than you can on the inside. Politicians, like journalists, seldom step up as bold leaders. They tend to wait until an idea is roaring down the tracks and then jump on the train. Or they wait until there is a crisis that just must be resolved.

If a private citizen is pushing and shoving and struggling in "the real world," that person often has a better grip on what's going on at ground level, what needs to be fixed and what needs to be done about it.

Take, for example, health care costs. It had become the biggest economic issue in the country by the turn of the new century in 2000. Hyperinflation over four decades had driven costs in that sector to 18 percent of GDP. The U.S. model for delivering care had become the number one cause of personal bankruptcy for Americans. By 2017, Milliman Consulting put the per family price tag at more than $28,000, with 44 percent landing on the shoulders of the worker.

15. Making Policy from the Ground Up

Further, the spiraling costs, rising at double digits annually, were crowding out strategic priorities, like K-12 and college education, defense, infrastructure investment, environmental initiatives, and even public safety.

Out-of-control health costs also were hammering business bottom lines. That was true at Serigraph. We were hemorrhaging in 2003 at $5.5 million in total health costs. The trends were worse. The company and its co-workers in 2003 were staring at a 15 percent projected increase in 2004. We didn't have another $800,000 for that benefit, so I decided that Serigraph would take the issue head-on. I soon discovered that solutions we found at Serigraph would apply in the broader economy.

By then, I had some spare time to take on such Don Quixote adventures. My very capable son Sean had moved up to chief operating officer, and he didn't need a lot of my help to run the core of the company. I needed to get out of his way.

With Sean carrying the heavy load, I had more time for the policy arenas that I cared about, including the crushing load of providing health care.

I had gone overboard in terms of serving on policy, civic, and non-profit boards. At one point, I was on 19 boards, way too many. I cut it back to 11. It was a great way to contribute, stay engaged, stay young in spirit and make like-minded friends.

That's how I became an ally of Mayor John Norquist of Milwaukee. As health costs sabotaged his city budget, he created a task force on health costs and asked me to co-chair it.

Curiously, I had once written a column labeling Norquist "a Scandinavian socialist." He called me the next day and thanked me. I hadn't exactly meant it as a compliment. We became respectful collaborators.

The mayor invited all the usual academic policy wonks and executives from the health care industry. They knew a lot about care, but had no answers on costs. It was about that time that I realized the business model for the delivery of health care in America was just plain busted.

A new business model had to be found, and I decided to make Serigraph an incubator for those new ideas. We had long been a self-insured company, underwriting our own health care risks. So, any savings we could generate would go right to our bottom line, not to an insurance pool.

In 2002, major corporations soon started to "disintermediate" health insurers, choosing to self-insure. That's Platform I, A deputy secretary of the U.S. Treasury, Roy Ramthun, had inserted a couple paragraphs in a Medicare repair bill that created Health Savings Accounts (HSAs) as a tax-advantaged device to help Americans with health care costs. (I later worked with him to protect HSAs when Obamacare went through Congress in 2010.) The HSAs, and their cousin, Health Reserve Accounts (HRAs), gave Serigraph a way to add incentives and disincentives to turn our people into serious consumers when they purchased health care. "It's the incentives, stupid!" one noted economist said.

On Jan. 1, 2004, we became an early mover toward a Consumer Directed Health Plan (CDHP). We raised our deductibles and offset them with a generous HRA. This reform worked right out of the gate. When anything is free or cheap, as with low deductible plans, people use too much of it. That overuse had caused much of the bloated U.S. health care bill. That's Platform II.

In speeches, I would recount that the Marine Corps officers' club served ten-cent martinis at Friday night happy hours, adding that I was occasionally over-served. Free or close-to-free anything leads to abuse and over-utilization.

15. Making Policy from the Ground Up

Utilization at Serigraph dropped 17 percent in the first six months after the CDHP change. Over-utilization was on the way out. We were on our way to a disruptive business model for the delivery of care. We now know from numerous national and longitudinal studies that CDHP plans save 20 to 30 percent of costs. The proven savings became beyond debate.

The next major platform for reform, Platform III, beyond self-insurance and CDHP, was to move away from the reactive care that characterized U.S. medicine ("We'll fix you when you're sick") to proactive care ("We'll keep you well and out of the hospital"). We went far beyond wellness brochures and websites to an on-site primary care clinic, headed by a nurse practitioner. It is what later became known as "a medical home."

In business terms, we took control of the front end of the supply chain for care. Our own contracted professionals were ordering lab tests, scans, prescriptions, specialists and hospital admissions, as opposed to the agents of the hospital corporations who over-order everything because they are incentivized to do so. The hospital corporations and collusive health insurers had become revenue obsessed. They had created the Medical-Industrial Complex (my term), similar to the Military-Industrial Complex that President Eisenhower had warned the nation about in the 1950s. (His "complex" had claimed 4 percent of GDP, versus health care at 18 percent.)

The smart move to proactive primary care improved the well-being of employees and also proved to save another 20 to 30 percent of total health bills.

Platform IV of Serigraph's drive was for value-based health care was bundled bills—a single, fixed price for procedures. This value-based purchasing became an antidote to incomprehensible, code-based medical bills that had long confused and plagued consumers.

To wit: my CFO and I could not figure out my 2005 bill for a hip replacement. How could any consumer? Those foggy bills with dozens of line items amounted to consumer fraud.

By 2016, Serigraph was buying joint replacements like mine for $26,000, all in, compared to $47,500 as a median in the Milwaukee marketplace and bills as high as $90,000. Such variations of 400 percent applied across most medical procedures and treatments. Lab tests varied 900 percent.

If Serigraph co-workers would select one of our value providers—high quality, good service, low infection rates, and low prices — we erased their charges for deductibles and co-insurance. Their procedures became free. *Shazam!* My new knee, which worked fine, was a freebie. The bundled price saved me $6,500 and the company $15,000.

Further, it was delivered at the Orthopedic Hospital of Wisconsin, a "lean" hospital with almost no readmissions to repair botched surgeries, low infections, and real missions. It was top rated in the U.S. I had learned that there is an inverse correlation in health care: the lower the prices, the better the outcomes.

Think about the magnitude of these innovations on a broader scale—collectively a new business model. I dubbed the new model "Value Health Care" in competition with Obamacare.

In 2016, Serigraph was delivering care for about $12,000 per employee. Kaiser News Service put the national average cost at $18,000. We were still at the 2016 level in 2020. In effect, we had taken the hyper-inflation out of health care.

If those numbers were extrapolated, a good trillion dollars could be taken out of the nation's bloated $3.8-trillion-plus health care bill. That would free up funds for education at all levels, for defense, for environmental advances, for infrastructure and public safety—and for universal health care coverage.

15. Making Policy from the Ground Up

The reforms spread across the private sector like a prairie fire. And the reforms engendered in the private sector crept into local government after 2010, because the economic pain was high there, too.

Ironically, that was the year the Affordable Care Act (ACA), known as Obamacare, was rammed through Congress. ACA did increase access, but did nothing to lower costs. Indeed, it raised costs in every part of the new law. Its title was Orwellian. It should have been called the Unaffordable Care Act.

Obamacare was a top-down, wonky, ham-handed political attempt at reform. In contrast, Value Health Care was bottom-up, pragmatic and market based. That doesn't mean that Value Health Care would win in the end. Lefty politics would use the collapse of ACA to move to Medicare-for-all as a fix. Republicans, dense on cost management, don't listen much to business friends. The GOP campaigned to "repeal and replace" ACA, but had no viable replacement plan—no Plan B. Both parties stayed bankrupt on health care policy, even into the 2020 presidential election campaigns. It was all about sound bites.

The Serigraph crusade propelled me into my fifth and sixth careers: author and speaker. (Aside: My first four careers were stints in the military, journalism, business, and a short encounter with government and politics. The seventh was to run an angel-investing fund.)

My two books on the new model (*The Company that Solved Health Care* in 2010 and *The Grassroots Revolution in Health Care* in 2013) sold more than 25,000 copies and became a roadmap for other employers. Royalties are a skimpy $1.50 per book.

As I previously mentioned, the first book led to a speaking tour across the country, allowing me to spread the word about the huge savings available from innovative management. It also allowed me to meet other innovators and gather material for the second book.

After 50 years of being grossly undercompensated as a journalist and author, I finally figured out where the gold was hidden. My speaker's bureau started me at $5,000 per talk, but then moved the fee up to $12,500 and finally $15,000. I worked hard at giving provocative speeches that communicated, and the word spread in the huge health care industry. It was not $250,000 per speech like Bill Clinton, but a lot better than the $50,000 per year I made as business editor of the *Milwaukee Sentinel* after more than 20 years in the business. I became a road warrior and gave two or three speeches a month to business leaders over a three-year period, earning more than $300,000.

I like to think I threw some gasoline and matches on the prairie fire of grassroots health-care reform.

Importantly, the innovative approach to health care and its costs proved popular with Serigraph employees and saved the company and its people more than $3 million per year against trend. Those savings helped enormously as the company fought to survive the Great Recession of 2007 to 2010, a business set-back in 2017 and 2018, and the Covid economic collapse of 2020.

By 2017, the national average for employee share on annual health care was around $5,000. Serigraph employees, who helped to manage our medical bills, were paying about $2,000. My Don Quixote fight to get US health costs, which were pushing toward 20 percent of the US economy, under some control continued to take about a third of my time. It was a fight worth fighting.

I often made the comment to potential angel investors that having 12 start-up companies in your portfolio is like have 12 teenagers in your house. An exaggeration, of course, but not too far off the mark for the Wisconsin Super Angel Fund, of which I was a general partner. A few entrepreneurs knew as much about starting a company as we did, but most needed our help, either as a board member or as a consultant.

Here are two of our war stories:

*****

Our best deal was one where we were just along for the ride. It was Phoenix Nuclear in Middleton WI, a company run by two nuclear physicists trained at the UW–Madison. They had invented a very high-voltage machine for extracting Moly 99, an isotope from the molybdenum molecule that is used broadly as a tracer in medical imaging.

Moly 99 was in short supply because linear accelerators were going obsolete and out of business. The market for Moly 99 is large and the demand is high. We joined with Madison venture investors we knew and invested $500,000 for 3 percent of Phoenix Nuclear.

We had no seats on the board, but it proved to be an ethical company, so our lack of control was never an issue. Our 3 percent was diluted to 2 percent as the company raised more capital to continue its growth. The company was worth about $17 million when we invested. Our 2 percent became worth $2.5 million when Phoenix merged into its biggest customer, Shine Medical, that extracted the Moly 99 using our neutron machines.

We decided to stay invested in Shine Medical, based on our assessment that it would go public in the not too distant future at a much bigger number.

*****

In 2005, health costs were killing Serigraph. We were spending $5.5 million per year and the inflation for 2016 was projected at 15 percent. The company simply could not afford that kind of increase. We needed a radical change on how we purchased insurance.

Because prices varied 400 percent from provider to provider, we start a sourcing campaign to buy directly from high quality clinics at fixed, low prices. Our first direct contract outside of our insurance network was with Smart Choice MRI for $487 per scan, compared to $3000 to $5000 in hospitals.

Our second direct buy was for joint replacements. A top quality, self-standing bone shop, led by a quality-obsessed surgeon, charged us $26,000 all-in. That compared to incomprehensible hospital bills that averaged $49,000.

Why would any company pay more than we were paying? Serigraph soon was saving $400,000 per year, about 10 percent of its medical treatment spend.

Eric Haberichter, the entrepreneur who started Smart Choice MRI, dreamed up a business model for taking "bundled prices" big time. His new company, Access Health Net (AHN), worked hard to assemble a network of enlightened providers who would trade lower fixed prices for more volume. He wanted to take it national by selling to self-insured employers like Serigraph.

My start-up fund, the Wisconsin Super Angel Fund, liked his guts and smarts, the size of the potential market, and the huge possible savings for many companies. We put in $500,000 in start-up capital in 2016 to get him up and running.

Even though the concept made sense and had been proven out, we had a hard time signing up customers. Working out of a big new office in downtown Milwaukee, Eric swung for the fences with a sharp staff of more than 20.

Our profits were to come from a 6 to 10 percent facilitation fee on every surgery or procedure we arranged. On paper, all looked great. One big potential deal after another got to the altar, but was never consummated. Still believing in the model and Eric, we put in another $205,000 in 2018, which took us to 5.5 percent of the company.

But what's a company without sales? AHN kept burning cash and sales never hit $20,000 per month. Tom Schuster, my fellow general partner in the fund, kept finding just enough new capital to keep AHN alive.

It was still running on fumes in 2021, but had a shiny object, a big new contract, just around the corner. Verdict? Still alive but prospects remained uncertain.

Starting a company, even with a proven concept and good people, is never easy.

EDITORIAL POSTSCRIPT

You learn that when taking on major issues, like out-of-control US health care costs, that it could take a decade or two to effect change. Good concepts take time to take root. Powerful forces will defend the lucrative status quo. But great ideas have power, and, in the end, good policy makes for good politics.

Patience and persistence are essential to success, whing are necessary to offset the inevitable concepts that fail. Similar efforts in the private sector, combined with downward pressure on some costs, did reduce the rate of health cost inflation by 2020.

Kine and I helped get the restoration going for the downtown theatre in our town. Four years and $4.6 million later, "The Bend" was once again an entertainment gem and gathering place for the community.

This sculpture "West Bend Resolve," created in 1995 by O. V. Shaffer, depicts the westerly bend of the Milwaukee River inverted. It is one of more than 40 pieces we placed along the river and in the city's parks. The collection has become a signature for the West Bend community.

CHAPTER 16

Social Entrepreneurship:
FIGHTING THE GOOD FIGHT ON THE HOME FRONT

Over a long career, made possible by a lucky and long life, blessed with the genetic gift of high energy, I was able to contribute in several dimensions: economic development, the arts, the environment. Lots of interests make for an engaged life and a long obituary, longer than anyone wants to read.

Best of all from my civic endeavors was the hundreds and hundreds of friends, good friends, made along the way, while working together for a common cause.

DOWNTOWN COMES ALIVE AGAIN

Work outside my job all started with Mowry Smith, an old Yale guy whose family owned the Menasha Corporation. He took me under his wing when I took over management of the newspaper in Neenah and Menasha. I was in my mid-20s, and he got me a board seat on the Menasha Redevelopment Corporation.

It was stimulating, because the central part of that blue-collar manufacturing town had run down as the strip malls drained commerce to the highways on the outskirts.

Menasha eventually developed a lovely marina downtown on a channel off the Fox River. And that project sparked other renovations and new buildings.

Later, when Post Corp. sent me to West Bend, its downtown was also challenged. The two hotels were defunct; the J.C. Penney Store had closed; the downtown movie theater was run down; the old milk condensery and grain elevator were empty hulks.

In 1970, a group of business men organized what would become the West Bend Urban Redevelopment Corp. and set about to breathe some new life into the downtown. Most of them gradually moved on, but I stayed with the complex project for 50 years.

We created a great public-private partnership, interacted with six different mayors and councils, and worked to keep the downtown viable and attractive. The condensery and grain elevator were taken down and eventually replaced by a fabulous Museum of Wisconsin Art, a shiny white triangular repository of regional art.

Early on, the partnership cleaned up a dozen contaminated brownfield sites. The most notable was the toxic West Bend Plating site next to the downtown dam. It was the site of dozens of early companies that helped the city grow. The last did electroplating, a dirty business that uses a brew of chemicals. We and the city worked hard with state and federal agencies for several years for an acceptable cleanup solution—to no avail.

One afternoon, I was looking over the nasty site with John Capelle, the brilliant city planner. He had invited an EPA regulator to get his input. The guy had grown up in nearby Kewaskum and had picked the project to get a trip back to his hometown. The plating building practically glowed in the dark. Though boarded up, it was a hazard, a magnet for mischievous kids. The EPA guy quietly asked me, "Would you like to see that building down?" I responded, "Hell, yes!"

16. Social Entrepreneurship

One week later, under an emergency order from the EPA, a crew removed the ugly structure. It just disappeared: he used Super Fund money, so there was no charge to the city. Then, the DNR and EPA finally agreed to a clay cap on the contaminated river bed. The site became an attractive park. The cleaned-up space was beautified by an earthwork sculpture called "Place of Origin" for all the companies that had started there, including the famous pots and pans manufacturer, the West Bend Aluminum Company.

People now catch edible fish below the dam.

A WORLD-CLASS SCULPTURE COLLECTION

In the early 1990s, I concluded after two decades living there that West Bend needed a signature. I had grown to love sculpture ever since my grad school days in Stockholm, the home of the re-nowned Milles Gardens, an enchanting fountain depiction of dancing Nordic fairies. Oslo had an equally compelling sculpture garden called Viegland Park, a display of stout, stoic humans.

I never had much artistic talent, but I liked the arts, especially 3D art. It had a permanence that was the exact opposite of the ephemeral newspapers I produced every day, relevant for no more than 24 hours.

There was always hope that some of my columns would inject ideas into the Wisconsin dialogue that would stick, but most were fleeting in impact. Sculptures had the chance of lasting a hundred years or more. It was appealing to be able to leave something behind. A group of us created West Bend Friends of Sculpture in 1992, with the simple goal of placing one or two major pieces of outdoor sculpture in the community every year.

We kept the group loose and informal, but with a serious purpose. Every meeting was a party, well supplied with wine. We made great friends, and, by 2018, we had more than 50 pieces in place, crafted by some of the best artists in the world.

Our role was that of impresario. We matched donors with sculptors and facilitated the placement of the pieces in the city. West Bend quietly but steadily became "The City of Sculptures."

The whole thing worked, partly because we tied the pieces to three historical themes: the connection to the Milwaukee River and its banks; the city's heritage of making objects in its manu-facturing plants, like sculpture is man-made; and the city's long-standing investment in its public parks, where many of the 3D works were sited. Most of our pieces had links to the city in one way or another.

It also worked because we retained Shawn Graff as our part-time executive director. He proved a brilliant rainmaker with a master's in art history.

We "friends" were always mindful of public relations; ours was public art, which can get controversial. One of our first pieces was *Fluvio*. Sculptor Paul Trappe outlined his shapes on two massive columns of Valders limestone with black markers and then invited the community to help him chip away the excess stone. Hundreds of citizens, including children, did their part. Trappe did the finishing work. *Fluvio* translates from Italian to "of the river," and it resides next to the Milwaukee River in Riverside Park. The massive horizontal top piece floats over a sea of native plants that grow happily in the river bottoms.

The projects were often boot-strapped, with help from many volunteers. The night the two slabs of granite arrived in down-town West Bend for the communal chip-off was nasty — windy, rainy and cold. West Bend Concrete lent us a monster forklift, but its rear wheels lifted off the ground as the operator tried to remove the three-ton slabs from the truck. Undaunted, he finally inched both heavy blocks off the flat-bed, and the project was underway. I was cold and soaked.

Fluvio could be there 100 years — or more — along with all its peers.

MILWAUKEE REPERTORY THEATER

Almost every time I join a board, it's crisis time. After I was recruited to the Rep board, I soon learned that subscriptions to its Powerhouse Theater, its main stage, were in free-fall. Attendance had dropped from a high point of 21,000 for the series of five performances to about 13,000.

Having been in the newspaper subscription business, I was alarmed.

I remember going to a play in that time frame called *The Torch*, an experimental play out of Brazil. It was so lame that my wife Pati and I climbed backward out of our seats to leave midway in the first half. We went to an adjacent bar, which was filled with fellow departees.

Sara O'Connor was general manager and John Dillon the artistic director. They had been together a decade and a half and after much success, had lost touch with audiences.

At a board meeting, I pointed to the mission of The Rep: "To illuminate the human condition." Say what?

I asked if entertainment were part of the mission. I got puzzled looks. I was a lone business voice on the board of the staff-driven organization. But we were in trouble, and everyone knew it. That enabled me to recruit a couple of sharp business people for the board.

First, I asked if we could stage some commercial plays. That did not go well with the high brows. Then, though, I came up with the right phrasing. "Could we stage some successful plays," such as those plays that had done well off-Broadway?

The pressure to come up with better offerings resulted in Dillon departing and the hiring of Joe Hanreddy, a brilliant young director who came up with a fresh slate that immediately lifted ticket sales.

Sara O'Connor also decided to move on, in her case to become a Buddhist monk. But, as she exited right, she agreed to take on an endowment campaign, something I had been pushing for from my first year on the board. We raised $12 million, and The Rep was solidly endowed for the future.

All's well that ends well.

My son Sean later joined the board and also served six years.

I learned a couple of things from The Rep experience. You are not a director to be a buddy of the executive team. You are there to help them deal with reality, to guide them to the high ground, to demand performance. Most directors just go along with staff direction or in-direction.

Second, most non-profit organizations need to get an endowment effort going. It can start slowly, but, over time, gives permanent sustenance to the organization.

Kine and I remained Rep season ticket holders, enjoying one of the best theater companies in America for many years.

16. Social Entrepreneurship

UNITED WAY STRIFE

A perfect example of the need to be assertive on a board occurred when I was campaign manager and a director of the United Way of Washington County.

The abortion issue was raging across the country, as it had for a half century and would continue for decades ahead. The conflict between Planned Parenthood and right-to-life groups, both recipients of United Way donations, was ripping apart United Way organizations across the US. Some folded as a result.

We were facing the same controversy in West Bend, and donors on both sides of the issue were threatening to cut off donations. Our board tried to duck the issue. But we had to deal with it, so I made the motion to remove both from our list of supported agencies.

"These two organizations have their own bases of passionate supporters," I argued. "They should go there to raise their own funds. They don't need United Way.

"Further, their fight could jeopardize our support of 16 other agencies, like the Scouts, the Red Cross and the food pantry.

"We need to be a 'vanilla' organization."

The motion narrowly passed.

GREEN AND GOLD AND SAVING THE NATURAL WORLD

You would think that growing up and coming of age in Wisconsin, the state with perhaps the longest heritage of conservation, would be a smooth ride for an environmentalist. It hasn't worked out that way, mainly because in the 2000s the Republican Party lost track of its roots in taking care of the country's natural resources.

Our family history made clear the imperative to take care of our planet. Great-grandfather Ludwig Torinus, who later changed his name to Louie, came to the United States at age 19 from the Ukraine in 1853 and found his way to the St. Croix River as a lumberman. He moved into business quickly, married a lumber baron's daughter, and started two lumber companies himself.

He and his competitors cut down the massive white pine forest like there would be no end. There was. It all came to an abrupt halt about 1910 when the "pinery" was gone and the land lay stripped. On a second pass, the hemlock was mowed down for its bark tannin for the leather business. My grandfather Burdette Torinus ran the family lumber camp near Ely, Minnesota.

With foresight, Wisconsin conservationists, including the paper companies, responded with reforestation. Today, half the state is forest, more than when Ludwig arrived, although many of the new trees were in what could be called plantations, not diverse forests.

The forward thinkers sent 12-year-old lads like me to "Trees for Tomorrow" camp. And the Boy Scouts taught us conservation principles. We grew up knowing we had to take care of the land, air, and water that take care of us.

Later in life, that core belief led Kine and me to get actively involved in the land trust movement, perhaps subconsciously making amends for Ludwig's and Burdette's transgressions. (L.E. Torinus actually owned Kine's sister's land on Little Bass Lake near Cable, Wisconsin, next door to where Kine and I owned a cabin that was our base for Nordic skiing.)

In Kine's case, the amends were for denuding of the forests along the Wisconsin River by the Kelly Lumber Co., owned by her forebears.

She and I helped launch the Ozaukee-Washington Land Trust (OWLT) in 1998. Its mission became the protection of the lands and waters along the Milwaukee River and its three branches and the shores of Lake Michigan. Kine became the third president of the trust and later interim executive director.

After she served the maximum ten years as a director, she asked me to take her place; I followed orders and did ten years. We were honored as the godmother and godfather conservationists of OWLT in 2017.

By then, the trust had protected more than 6,000 acres of sensitive lands.

The land trust movement in Wisconsin grew as fast as we were growing, reaching 45 trusts across the state. It had the fervor of a religious movement.

I had the added privilege of being elected to the board of the Wisconsin Chapter of The Nature Conservancy (TNC), the biggest environmental organization in the world. TNC does the big projects that the local land trusts can't handle. And it preaches and practices science-based approaches to conservation.

Elected later as chapter chairman, I pushed TNC to do more. By and large, TNC stays in the uncontroversial background, avoiding leadership roles.

I tried to move TNC executives to take the lead on a master plan for protecting the Great Lakes. My concept was to have local land trusts each monitor and clean up their local tributaries to the lakes. They would be the boots on the ground, while TNC would orchestrate a master plan across eight states and two Canadian provinces. It would also contribute science. Despite high-level, multi-state conferences on the subject, I never made the sale. TNC did not want the accountability that comes with leadership.

I joked, "TNC's strategy is raising tons of money." It pulls in half a billion dollars per year, which it can deploy for protecting big parcels, such as those divested by the paper companies starting in the 1990s. The donations also support a big league bureaucracy, which, like all bureaucracies, works hard to preserve itself.

That sardonic view aside, we need all the positive contributions that can be mustered to protect our natural resources from the pressures of a growing population. The Republican Party posed major threats in the new century, tilting toward extraction over protection. Democrats moved toward the other extreme.

I wrote dozens of columns and blogs to the effect that both the environment and the economy can be accommodated with a collaborative model for regulation. That's how they do it in Sweden, where I did my master's degree in political science. Every affected party gets a seat at the policy-making table. Here, partisan politics often block good policy.

Close to home, we walked the talk at Serigraph. We proved that it is possible to be good stewards of both the company and our piece of the earth.

Our company developed a biofilter, the first in the world, to oxidize the solvents in our air emissions, our company's main form of pollution. The biofilter removed more than 90 percent of our volatile organic compounds.

In addition, we recycled almost all our solid waste, reduced our water use by half and captured run-off pollution in a sediment pond before it flowed into the Milwaukee River. The native prairie at our headquarters has been a work of art in four seasons.

Serigraph's environmental management system became ISO 14000 certified, and we became the second of only three companies in Wisconsin to win a Green Tier II contract from the state and the EPA. It took a painfully long six years to get state and federal agencies to certify our biofilter.

Our environmental advances cost the company very little in relation to our total costs. So why wouldn't we be green and gold? (Note: The successful Packer colors.)

There are benefits in other dimensions. Employees like to work for a green company, and some customers require ISO 14000.

In short, good stewardship is good business.

MOVING UW–MILWAUKEE TO WORLD CLASS

It should be a given that the once-great University of Wisconsin system draws full support from taxpayers and legislators. But, by the turn of the century, that was not the case.

Often its own worst enemy, the Madison-centric UW System got itself crosswise with conservatives and leaders of the Republican Party. That, plus state budget problems compelled Democratic and GOP leaders to slash UW budgets from 2000 on. It became a bipartisan funding cut-back.

I tried to help reposition UW in the hearts and minds of citizens and leaders by serving on commissions and writing blogs and columns of support of higher investment in post-secondary education.

One assignment was to chair a commission in 2006 on the future of the UW's 13 two-year community colleges. West Bend was home to one of the thirteen, the University of Wisconsin-Washington County. The colleges offer a great start to place-bound students. UWWC then had 1,000 students, who benefited from a low-budget way to do the freshman and sophomore years.

Through the commission, I enjoyed creating a productive dialog with University leaders, faculty, students, business, the technical colleges and political leaders. We used a unique iterative process. We would write a draft of each chapter as the facts and evidence unfolded in public sessions. It took a lot of tenacity to work through the complex issues on how the 13 colleges would interact with the 13 UW four-year colleges and the 47 campuses in the Wisconsin Technical College System.

We had many policy recommendations, but two really took hold and worked well:

- Freeze tuition at the colleges to maintain a lower price point for college entry.

- Endorse a "university center" plan that delivered baccalaureate degrees from the four-year colleges on the two-year campuses.

Both took root in public policy and helped students. The center concept was later dropped, a victim of university politics and short-sightedness.

Go, UWM Panthers!

If ever a city and region needed a strong university, it would be Milwaukee. The city and southeastern Wisconsin were hit hard by the decline of the Rust Belt from about 1980 on as manufacturing jobs, once the core of the regional economy, melted away in the face of increased productivity, automation, industrial consolidation, off-shoring, lean disciplines and global competition.

Good-paying middle-class jobs in the central city gave way to all those forces and to single-story plants in the suburbs. Gone were big factories in the city like those of Allis-Chalmers, Rexnord, Allen-Bradley, Schlitz, Blatz, Pabst, Crucible Steel and A.O. Smith.

That erosion triggered a downward spiral in the central city of unemployed men, fatherless homes, high birth rates to single mothers, segregation, drug trafficking and nightly gun violence.

16. Social Entrepreneurship

Yet the Milwaukee downtown itself stayed relatively healthy, due to corporate offices there. But the rest of the City of Milwaukee suffered.

How to break out of the conundrum?

One obvious answer was to transform the University of Wisconsin–Milwaukee from a second-rate "access" university to a world-class urban university. UWM had long been a PhD-granting institution, with 850 professors in 13 colleges and nearly 30,000 students. It had the potential to be a powerhouse.

I supported its transformation efforts. Three brilliant chancellors set the vision: Nancy Zimpher, who later became president of the New York university system; Carlos Santiago, who became Zimpher's provost in New York; and Mike Lovell, who left to become president of Marquette University.

They all chafed at the lack of support for UWM from governors, legislators, including those from the Milwaukee region, and UW System leaders. UWM always got the short end of the funding stick in comparison to UW–Madison, the state's fabulous flagship research university. Per student support was less than half of Madison's.

Unfortunately, UW–Madison does not engage the state effectively beyond the borders of liberal Dane County. Its mission should always be to propel the whole state toward prosperity. It does send its graduates across the state. Serigraph hired some of them. But other positive impacts on the state as a whole were minimal.

In my view, that's not enough of an impact for the flagship campus. UW–Madison ducked the poverty issues in Milwaukee. It ducked statewide issues including rural poverty and public health.

It sat self-contented in the oasis of Dane County and in the limelight of basic research like stem cell breakthroughs and patents.

In 2006, while Santiago was chancellor, I was asked to be the first chairman of a new UWM Research Foundation (UWMRF). We sought and got a no-fault divorce from WARF, the famous Wisconsin Alumni Research Foundation that was endowed at the $3 billion level from licenses on such research breakthroughs as Vitamin D, Coumadin and stem cells.

There was no alimony, so it seemed folly to walk away from WARF's patronage. But the bureaucrats in Madison were not getting the job done in Milwaukee. UWM had one patent registered—850 professors and one patent. We were getting lip service from WARF on technology transfer.

We obtained a small amount of start-up money from the small UWM Foundation and from other local foundations and industries. We signed a contract with UWM for $200,000 to provide patent and license services. We hired Brian Thompson, a brilliant engineer who understood business and technology. He was the right choice.

Flash forward twelve years, and we had more than 120 patents approved for UWM faculty and grad students, 46 patents pending, a dozen licenses, and 17 start-ups launched from UWM technology. We accelerated to 60 to 75 disclosures of intellectual property per year. We had a staff of six, and we had lift-off as a research university, alongside our access mission for low-income students. In 2015, UWM was named a Carnegie R1 university, one of the top 115 research schools in the country.

I advocated for UWM to become "E-University" — Entrepreneurship University — to marry the seemingly incompatible missions of access and research. Every business needs the technology innovators, but also the people who know how to hustle in the marketplace. The latter could often be the access students: immigrants, veterans, minorities, and first-generation college attendees.

Through UWMRF, the campus made strong connections with the region's technology leaders at companies like WE Energies, Rockwell, JCI and GE Healthcare. The partnerships with industry would prove to be a major differentiator and source of long-term support for UWM.

THE PANTHER PROMOTERS

Because UWM was fighting a losing battle for state support, I teamed with a group of business experts in public relations and government relations in 2017 to drum up a coalition of heavy hitters to promote UWM.

We called ourselves the "Panther Promoters," named after the school's mascot. We created a strategic framework — a compelling story — that UWM was missing.

It had to be an external group, because Chancellor Mark Moore and his staff had to play inside baseball with the UW System staff. We didn't have to play their game. We would go straight to business leaders, the media, the governor, the regents and the legislators.

Part of our effort was to get the Democratic lawmakers in the city to work together with the Republican lawmakers in the suburbs. They rarely agreed, except when it came to raising a $250 million subsidy for the Milwaukee Bucks.

If the Bucks could pull major money from Madison with bipartisan support, why not UWM?

The seasoned Panthers team had decades of experience at influencing public opinion and policy. We knew the ins and outs of regional and state politics, how to handle the media, who to line up as campaigners and where to raise the money for the UWM cause. I was happy to be one of those geezers.

UWM finally got a fair share of UW funds in 2018 at $80 million for two building upgrades. It also won a new $120 million chemistry building for 2019-2021 and similar new engineering building for 2021–2023. Our lobbying of UW regents and key legislators could have paid off handsomely over time. Cranes would rise once more over the UWM campus.

Unfortunately, Chancellor Mark Moore and his team didn't like to rock boats with the regents and legislature in 2021. The ….were pulled from the Promoters' advocacy campaign, UWM reverted to second-class ranks in state fundraising, despite its lead as an access university from 6,700 students of color. Endemic discrimination—unconstitutional discrimination?

The Panther Promoters folded.

Save "The Bend"

A capstone project in 2017 at the end of a half century of leading and prodding downtown redevelopment was a campaign to restore, renovate and preserve the defunct West Bend Theatre.

The old vaudeville and "talkie" movie palace built in 1929 had gone dark in 2006. It had succumbed to competition from a 10-screen multiplex theater.

Its hollowed-out art deco shell sat right in the middle of our town on Main Street. The only sign of life in the old girl was the still-lit marquee that spelled out the words "West Bend" vertically in 470 white lights. It was an iconic symbol of the community. The building and the sign had to be saved.

16. Social Entrepreneurship

Kine and I agreed to step in as leaders. The enthusiasts for the restoration had little experience in building and running organizations, and the effort was in disarray.

We had played a similar role in 2016 by helping "Bike-Friendly West Bend" get up and running. We led by organizing the group under a non-profit corporation, getting the right people on the bus, identifying the leaders and drafting a strategic plan.

Within a few months, that new biking organization was performing very well, starting with new bike racks downtown and the demarcation of safe routes in a master plan of roads and trails.

Kine stayed on the board, and I backed off.

We decided to play the same role for Historic West Bend Theatre Inc. (HWBT). The group was stalled, undermined by internal and external controversy.

Kine gave the initiative credibility by signing on as vice president, and I went on the board. We acted as the volunteer executive directors.

Within months, we had recruited a passionate new board of young movers and shakers. We had signed up 1,700 supporters on social media. We drafted a business plan. We organized seven working task forces. And we had cut a deal to buy the facility.

After a market survey, our volunteer board was determined to fill the theatre with classic movies, musical gigs, live plays from local thespian groups, the Kettle Moraine Symphony, and events like reunions and corporate meetings.

We were going to light up the town. The theatre was to become the capstone of 50 years of community work to restore the river and the downtown. We raised $4.6 million over two years. Our project was a go. Construction kicked off in early 2019.

By March 2020, the theater had been restored as a masterpiece. The Grand Opening on March 14 was a roaring success. A hallmark was the discovery of enchanting stenciled artwork that had been covered with purple paint. With local artist Chuck Dwyer, we brought them all back to life.

Our timing was tragic in one sense. We were forced to close the next day to prevent the spread of pandemic caused by coronavirus COVID-19.

In another sense, we built the masterpiece when it was still possible to raise the funds and would be raring to go when the pandemic closures lift.

Editorial Postscript

Kine and I developed a philosophy for growing older. We would never retire. We would continue to contribute until we had nothing left to give. As "octos" — octogenarians — we found we still had a lot to offer for exciting initiatives. And we always got more than we gave.

16. Social Entrepreneurship

The 2021 donation to West Bend Friends of Sculpture, "The Bird," will perch downtown right on the east bank of the Milwaukee River. Sculpted by Sheila Berger, the stainless-steel piece will command the attention of everyone using the city's Riverwalk.

Paul Trappe of Australia conceived this limestone piece and outlined its form. Hundreds of volunteers from the community did the rough chipping to give it shape. "Fluvio" floats over a sea of wild flowers in Riverside Park.

Serigraph and Its People

- Our people come first.

- An employee's first obligation if to his or her family.

- Personal satisfaction and work go together.

- Our company must help its people to grow to their fullest potential, regardless of race, color, creed, national origin, gender, age, or sexual orientation.

- Decisions should be made in natural work units. We ask our people: "Help run our company."

- Employee involvement is the best way of meeting the company's challenges.

- A spirit of partnership between owners, management, and employees is the heart of the enterprise. Profit-sharing is part of that partnership.

- Rigorous educational and training opportunities are necessary for maintaining the long-term competitive advantage of a world-class work force.

- We will promote from within wherever possible.

- We will operate in an atmosphere of experimentation and creativity. We will take business risks.

- The employees and the company are best served in an alcohol-free, drug-free, smoke-free place of work where wellness and personal welfare are emphasized.

Every company has a culture, often implicit. I chose to make our beliefs explicit at Serigraph. Here is the section on our relations with our co-workers

CHAPTER 17

Fun and Un-Fun on 50 Boards

MAKING THE TOUGH CALLS

B y the time I hit 80, I had served on more than 50 boards of directors, two-thirds for non-profit corporations and one-third for-profit and still served on seven. It was mostly a privilege and pleasure to serve, but there were times when toughness was the order of the day.

I had always advised my sons of the need to be gentlemen, but to have a reserve of toughness. "Be as tough as you need to be, but no tougher."

Another of my bromides: "Save me from nice guys," the leaders who won't face realities and won't make the needed tough calls.

When I became embroiled in challenges or difficult issues that arose in organizations that I served, I often wondered, "Why me?" Most directors take a duck when confronting sticky challenges, even though they may constitute a business, legal or moral necessity. Over the years, I figured out why. Many business people in larger corporations rise in their careers by playing it safe, by not taking stand-up positions, by being political. So, when they are sitting in a board room, that's what they do when the proverbial stuff hits the fan. They sit back and keep their heads down, rather than lead.

I didn't go looking for board fights. On most of my board tenures, there was no need to confront a really tough issue. When they did arise, though, my nature was to never take a pass. If you are an entrepreneur or an editor, you have it in your DNA to take on difficult issues. So, I was either nominated — or self-nominated — to do so.

The hard issues always make for the best news copy, so let's start with those.

I only got sued as a director once and only got fired once.

The suit came after 16 years on a private company board in Green Bay. An aggrieved female manager sued the whole board for lack of fiduciary oversight in settlements with women in the company who had alleged sexual harassment by a senior executive.

The suit brought to light a pattern of such earlier settlements. Another director and I pushed through a strong anti-sexual harassment policy that clearly prohibited any romantic relationship between a superior and a subordinate.

Even with the new policy in place, the behavior continued. I had had it. I resigned. Several other directors followed me out the door.

The board was not really in the legal line of fire, and the outside lawyer we hired to represent the directors got the suit dropped.

It was too bad to have to quit. It was an excellent company otherwise and good place to learn best practices.

In the case of getting fired, it occurred after a CEO ran his company in West Bend into the rocks of bank foreclosure. Several investors and I called an emergency meeting, installed an outside board, and brought in a turn-around executive.

With the CEO parked in a small subsidiary where he could do no further damage, we worked with the troubled loan pros at the bank to forestall foreclosure. Our turn-around pro had the company back in the black in five months.

Then things got bizarre. The displaced CEO used an outdated operating agreement to throw out the whole board and put himself back in charge. Several directors started a legal action over shareholder suppression, but backed away from the legal expenses when they realized they were fighting over an enterprise with no real value.

Six years later, the company was still essentially insolvent, vulture lenders were in charge and the shareholders were out of luck. The CEO's family members were still taking out large salaries. It was a very unfun episode as a director. Early investors will never see a return.

MOSTLY POSITIVE OUTCOMES FROM GOOD BOARDS

Fortunately, the bad chapters in my tenure on boards were far outweighed by the positive experiences. Most directors are seasoned professionals and have much to offer to executive teams.

The executives have to drive the bus, but it's easy to veer or drift off path in a complex and ever-changing business world. Good boards can help a company set a more sure path toward its success.

As I got into angel investing, my fund made it a rule that we would not put our money into a start-up venture that did not have a seasoned board. Whenever we violated that practice, shareholder value suffered.

My son and I always regarded our board as one of our most valuable assets. They helped us through many dangerous twists and turns, gave us credibility and offered tips that directly saved us millions.

Like any other asset, especially human assets, directors need to be engaged by the executives. They need to be part of the action.

I liked to think I helped in all cases when serving as a director.

Two examples were Endries Fasteners, a distributor of low-cost industrial parts, and Placon Corp., a thermoformer of plastic packaging, both with about $100 million in sales. Both had aging CEOs, entrepreneurs who were nervous about turning over their creations to their sons. They asked me to evaluate their offspring in an objective way.

In both cases, after a year on their boards, I was able to convince the fathers that the sons were more than ready. The transitions went smoothly.

At Placon, I quickly determined that it had bloated inventories. That, plus a huge loan to buy out the father's stock, had made the balance sheet unstable. At my first meeting, I diplomatically asked why there was $16 million of inventory on the books. (My larger manufacturing company of similar size had less than half that level.)

I was told, "We make to forecast." That meant they were, in effect, selling to their warehouse.

At subsequent meetings, I continued to raise the subject. "Can't you make to order? Do you use lean manufacturing techniques, so you can make to order? If you transition to just-in-time manufacturing, couldn't you turn inventory dollars into cash dollars?"

Son Dan Mohs got the message and shifted gears. Inventory steadily dropped to $7 million, raising cash and bringing debt down by $9 million. The balance sheet was healthy again.

That enabled the company to launch three strategic initiatives, including two acquisitions. I decided to leave the board when I turned 75. Though asked to stay beyond the company's age limit, I decided to leave, mainly because the new CEO wasn't really listening to the board any more, and most of the board was comprised of family members.

THE BEST WAY TO RUN A BOARD MEETING

An essential tool in business, including at the board level, is mastery of dialogue. You get a bunch of smart people in a room, preferably from different disciplines, and you tackle a complex problem with an exchange that is fact-based, respectful, candid, hard-edged. Everyone is expected to contribute.

The solutions that emerge are invariably better than those from a single genius.

As Clayton Christianson, a business guru, sees it, the downfall of great corporations comes when they get arrogant, when they lose their humility, when they have the answers, not the questions. He defined humility as the willingness to learn.

When I chaired boards, I limited the agenda to the big strategic puzzles facing the organization. I would then stimulate the dialogue by asking tough questions.

At the beginning of every Serigraph board meeting, I asked the CEO, my son, "What are the three things keeping you up at night?" Then we spent the bulk of the board meeting on those issues. We did not "report at" the board with the facts and figures already contained in the board book, which we expect the directors to have read.

Invariably, the board's wisdom helped the CEO find a more effective way forward.

TOMMY'S RANT

One of my liveliest episodes as a chairman came when I was heading the Wisconsin Taxpayers Alliance, a long-standing, non-partisan analyst of tax trends in the state.

We had been publishing pieces that showed Wisconsin was in the top three states for the combination of state and local taxes as a percentage of per capita income—not a good place to be.

The state's leaders had historically followed a Germanic tradition of investment in education at all levels and in local roads and highways. That required the high taxes that went with those investments.

Our analysis did not sit well with Gov. Tommy Thompson, the state's leading cheerleader. He loved to start his speeches:

"Isn't it a great day to be in Wisconsin? Our kids have the highest ACT and SAT scores. Our exports are up. Unemployment is down. The Badgers are going to the Rose Bowl, and the Green Bay Packers are going to the Super Bowl."

Thompson was an unabashed optimist, and he was an excellent executive.

So, he fumed at our even-handed realism and demanded to meet our full board of directors. I invited him to do so.

Governor Thompson stormed into the meeting, launched into his theatrics and tried to put our board on the defensive.

The other directors were somewhat cowed, but I had been confronted as a journalist by any number of politicians unhappy about what had been reported. I listened respectfully and told him that we were going to have to continue to call the state's economic metrics like we saw them. I thought I saw an amused smile on his face as we arrived at a truce of sorts and he departed.

Tommy went on to win an unprecedented four terms as governor, and he appointed me to two blue ribbon commissions, one on workforce development and one on stimulating exports. I had a hand in writing and editing both white papers.

Wisconsin finally got out of the top ten for taxes in 2016, but continued to lag the nation in key economic metrics like wages, GDP growth, job growth and per capita income. Later, under Governor Scott Walker, the unemployment rate dipped to only three percent. Out-migration and a tight labor supply contributed.

Wisconsin's best growth years, when it moved up in national prosperity rankings, came during the Thompson years. He led the nation in welfare reform, combining subsidies with work in a W2 (Wisconsin Works) program. His welfare reforms went national and then international.

He later went on to become Secretary of Health and Human Services under President George W. Bush and ran unsuccessfully for president in 2012. He called me from that campaign trail: "John, I'm in Iowa and I need money." I wrote him a mid-sized check. He would have been a competent president.

BE BOLD — THE WISCONSIN PROSPERITY STRATEGY

Because I had been president of an organization called Competitive Wisconsin, a labor-management collaboration, I helped to organize four economic summits on cures for the lagging Wisconsin economy from 2000 to 2003 and another blue ribbon commission in 2010.

The summits were called by University of Wisconsin System President Katharine Lyall, a labor economist. We had become friends in a discussion group of economists and business leaders called the Keynes Society and while serving on her workforce commission.

Her instinct was to place the UW at the center of leadership on improving the state's economy. She was right on. Universities were becoming engines of growth in what came to be called "The Innovation Economy" or "The Knowledge Economy."

Several ideas from those summits stuck. One was to emphasize policies that propelled our economic "clusters," like manufacturing, agri-business and biotechnology. Another was to create angel investing groups across the state to stimulate a wave of high growth start-ups. Those took hold.

The best piece of start-up policy came in the form of Act 255, which offered a 25 percent tax credit to investors in high growth Wisconsin ventures.

Later, when I edited and wrote parts of the 2010 "Prosperity Strategy," I made sure that those themes carried through. Thirty of the state's major stakeholder groups signed onto that economic blueprint. Again, it centered on clusters and start-ups. It boldly called for $1 billion in state start-up investments. Our governor and legislative leaders dribbled in $25 million in 2014.

Of necessity, private leaders picked up the mantle. Another guy and I, with support from the state's largest utility, headed up the launch of BizStarts Milwaukee, a non-profit organization that created a support system for entrepreneurs.

Once that infrastructure was up and running, I jumped over to the for-profit side to create a badly needed pool of capital to invest in start-ups. Wisconsin Super Angels Fund, which invested $8 million in 12 high-growth start-ups, made good use of the 25 percent tax credit.

The momentum for startups grew from those early efforts. By 2020, venture capital investment in Wisconsin had grown to more than $400 million per year. The $100 million level of state investment came up again in 2021 in Governor Evers' budget, but the Republican legislature axed it.

17. Fun and Un-Fun on 50 Boards

Editorial Postscript

When asked to join a board, I always said, "Don't put me on your board if you don't want an active director." You are there to help with the main challenges facing the enterprise, even though some owners want "yes-men" boards.

Serigraph's series of directors over the years were invaluable. Our job was to make sure they were engaged properly to get the best value from them. View your board as an enormous asset.

Never invest in a company that doesn't have a strong board. Proactive governance of other people's money is an absolute requirement for a healthy business.

Kine and I were most comfortable in the outdoors of Wisconsin. On occasion we dressed up and hit the social circles.

CHAPTER 18

On Growing Old Gracefully:
THREE GOLDEN RULES, 15 FREEDOMS

H ere is a haiku from brother Tom on old age:

> *From here in the front row,*
> *the view is infinite.*

As friends regale me with their long lists of ailments, I sometimes say, "Congratulations! You accomplished your goal — you grew old. What did you think it would be like when you got there?"

Despite physical limitations, if you are in reasonably good health, it's a blessing to grow old, as Kine and I were able to do so together. It's a blessing because you suddenly have the time, resources, hopefully wisdom and inclination to bless and contribute to the lives of those around you — your family several generations deep, your friends, your community, your state, and your country.

THE FIRST GOLDEN RULE

To my way of thinking, the trick for healthy, happy chapters late in life is that sense of continuing contribution, which, in turn, means engagement with the world, with old friends and new acquaintances. It is the antidote to the dreaded disease of old age: loneliness.

When my snowbird friends would come back to Wisconsin from their winter hibernations in Florida or Arizona, I would sometimes jest, "Please don't talk about a) the weather, b) your golf game, or c) your ailments." The conversation would often go dead.

When most retired, they often disengaged from most of their previous activities, not just their jobs. Therefore, they had little else to talk about.

Jokingly, I would ask: "Did you hear the harp music down there in Florida, God's little waiting room?" It wasn't funny for them, so I stopped being a smart ass.

So, when you get out of bed in the morning and you say to yourself: "It's not about me," the ailments fade from mind as you get on with engagements outside your own needs.

I primed myself every morning by saying my own haiku: "Ooh Rah" (Let's make something good happen today); "Tak Tak" (thanks for another day of life and previous blessings); "Ha Ha" (Let's have some fun today); and "Not about me." I later added as I hit the age of grumpiness: "Be nice."

I could never agree with the concept of "retirement." The word implies withdrawal from many things that went before. Bad idea. The concept should be "redirection" from one set of efforts to another. Perhaps to civic or charitable work; perhaps to another career; perhaps to a serious hobby that helps others; perhaps to help with kids or grandkids.

But the notion of retiring to a life of self-indulgence makes neither philosophical, psychological, religious, nor economic sense. All religions praise contribution. All thinkers extol an engaged life.

Further, our society cannot afford to subsidize adults from retirement at 55, 60 or 65 to the new life expectancy of about 80. We all are going to have to work and contribute for more years, especially with longer lives and a shrinking of the work force in the younger age groups.

18. On Growing Old Gracefully

THE TIM NIXON RULE

The second golden rule for old age is my Tim Nixon Rule. My dear friend of five decades was afflicted by throat and lower tongue cancer, and survived it with chemo, radiation, and surgery to remove much of his tongue and adjacent muscles.. He lost his ability to swallow and to talk clearly. All nourishment came through a tube to his stomach.

It never stopped him from full participation in the life around him. He took his tube and food bags to the golf course, to duck and pheasant hunts, and to parties. He cooked dinner for his wife Alice and friends, even though he could not partake. I asked him how he endured. He said simply, "John, I don't worry about what I can't do; I do what I can do."

And, of course, he finds plenty to do, including responding smartly to my weekly blog offerings, often with an interesting slant.

Tim occasionally imbibes a whiskey Manhattan at cocktail hour through his stomach tube. He joins the party.

THIRD GOLDEN RULE

The third golden rule is to stay mentally and physically active. Everyone knows that to be true, but many friends self-impose age-ism in the both realms. They stop exercising, even walking, and, worse, stop learning.

Yes, you give up high-impact sports as you age. It is sad to give up the sports you love, one by one, football first, then basketball, volleyball, mogul skiing, aggressive tennis, and finally skiing altogether.

But Kine and I kept at the low-impact sports — cross-country skiing, cycling, hiking, canoeing, and snowshoeing — until late in life. No more marathons, but we could do events of two to three hours until our late 70s, and finally an hour or two hiking the Ice Age Trail. Kine had to give up golf because of tendon issues; I took Ibuprofen and kept on playing, albeit from the white tees.

It helped that I was never an athlete of great distinction, so my expectations were never high. Unless you are a superstar, sports are just part of life, not the center of life. And participating is far more fun than spectating.

One of the best of times came at 71, when I joined an elder's team of eight in the famous "Bicycle Race Across America." It was a relay sprint, one rider at a time, day and night. We made it from Oceanside, California, near my old Marine base, to Annapolis, Maryland in seven days and 13 hours. How good is that? That was my biggest physical challenge ever.

The human body and brain literally shrink from under-use. Kine and I prodded each other to stay active and delay that process as long as possible. The big payoff from a life of exercise comes in the golden years when you can still do some of the things you like to do. Your muscles still respond pretty well.

One of the ironies of old age is that growing old is freeing in many ways. Think about all the challenges of life that no longer apply, about these latter-day freedoms, with tongue in cheek:

1. Freedom to say largely whatever you want to say in a straight-forward, respectful way without worrying too much about what someone might think about what you think or write.

2. The famous freedom to wear purple, to being who you are.

18. On Growing Old Gracefully

3. Freedom from ambition, having been there, done that.

4. If you were lucky and frugal, freedom from financial stress and the great pressure "to make it."

5. Freedom to be generous for your causes. What are you saving your reserves for if your children are set in life?

6. Freedom from character development. You are already a character.

7. Freedom from existential questions. Right or wrong, most elders have pragmatically sorted out the big issues, including the God issue, for themselves.

8. Freedom from educational imperatives and costs. Just study what you want to know. Go deeper on what you love and are good at — in my case, journalism.

9. Freedom from the responsibilities of child-raising. I enjoyed every inch of being a father to my two "boys." But you can play a delightful bit part in raising the grandkids. I enjoyed being "Bad Grandpa," such as: "Rules are for other people." You have a huge imprint on the youngsters.

10. Freedom from parental approval — though your spouse sometimes fills in for the departed parents.

11. Freedom from the most urgent of sexual drives, tensions, expectations. You can be another kind of lover.

12. Freedom from job descriptions, accountabilities, demands, except those you choose to take on.

13. Freedom from athletic competition. Who cares anymore? Just play. Just keep shooting, you might hit something. Don't keep score in golf if you don't want

to. In hunting, my brothers coined the phrase: "Shoot and release."

14. Freedom to take extended time off, not so much for indulgent pleasures, but for purposeful adventures—maybe a trip with a grandchild.

15. Freedom to mentor. Experience counts in many parts of life. Some younger people welcome help in avoiding the mistakes you made.

Long before retirement age, I came to the conclusion that I would never retire. I would stay engaged in real life as long as possible. That means writing new chapters in your book of life; call it reinventing yourself.

A 2016 study proved that the longer you work, the longer you live. I believe that.

If you stay physically, mentally, emotionally, and philosophically engaged, your golden years can be among your best.

Family Photos

Dad ("Tor") was formidable on stiff wooden skis.

I preferred an old-style "reverse shoulder" technique for pretty turns.

We skied at Aspen, CO, many springs after guests had departed from brother Chuck's "Applejack Inn." (L to R: Pati, John, Sean, Dan Torinus)

221

Coming to the finish line in one of 30 "Birkies" and half-Birkies, called the Kortelopet.

It's always smart to save some energy so you can look good coming to the finish line and the cameras of a cross-country ski race. I finished the 1984 52-Birkie in 4:41, as always a very average time.

The four Torinus brothers hunted together for decades on an annual trek to Saskatchewan. We never used guides, preferring to do our own scouting. Brother Mark (right) was our chief scout and the most fun.

Kine loved and excelled at cycling.

Best of times:
Biking together in Maine.

Kine was always a real-life "tree-hugger."

Kine and I made a compact to grow old together gracefully. It is a blessing to have a partner with whom to absorb the tough times that are inevitable in later years.

My Best Legacy

From L: John Torinus IV (Jack), Michael, John III (Sean), Cathie, and Sophia.

From L: Dan Torinus, Ingrid Klass Torinus, and Molly.

About the Author

John Torinus Jr. has worked as a journalist, entrepreneur, and business manager since leaving the U.S Marine Corps, where he served as an artillery company commander. John served 20 years as CEO of Serigraph Inc., a graphics parts manufacturer with four plants in West Bend, Wisconsin. He continues as its active chairman. John serves as a director for eight companies/non-profit organizations. He is the current treasurer of the UW–Milwaukee Research Foundation, as well as a general partner of the Wisconsin Super-Angel Fund, an angel investing fund. John has served on several task forces to reform health care delivery. He holds a baccalaureate in industrial administration from Yale and a master's degree in international relations from the University of Stockholm. Torinus, a former columnist and editor for Milwaukee newspapers, writes a blog on business, economics, and politics and a column for his hometown paper.

Website/Blog: www.johntorinus.com

dd724433-d5c7-4851-bda0-69f2fab24470R01